Non-Fiction for the Literacy Hour

Non-Fiction for the Literacy Hour

Classroom Activities for Primary Teachers

Guy Merchant and Huw Thomas

David Fulton Publishers
London

David Fulton Publishers Ltd,
Ormond House, 26–27 Boswell Street, London WC1N 3JZ

www.fultonpublishers.co.uk

First published in Great Britain by David Fulton Publishers 2001

British Library Cataloguing in Publication Data
A catalogue record for this book is available from the British Library

ISBN 1–85346–720–0

Typeset by FiSH Books, London
Printed in Great Britain by Bell & Bain Ltd, Glasgow

Contents

Acknowledgements

Acknowledgement is made to the following people/companies for permission to use copyright material:

Sheffield Recreation for advert for Graves Park Animal Farm

UCI Cinemas for *How the Projector Works*

Ferrero UK for the Galacteenies advert

The Office of National Statistics for *This is Your Census!*

Aladdin Books Ltd for *How do I feel about Bullies and Gangs?*, by Julie Johnson

Times Supplements for Ted Wragg's *Talking Points*

Sheffield Newspapers Ltd for 'Historic Eyam' from *The Star Family Walks*

The Contributors

We would like to acknowledge the contribution of those who have assisted with the collection and selection of texts, who have trialled activities and offered their professional advice and guidance at various stages in the development of this project.

Cathy Burnett, formerly a literacy consultant in Derby, now working in the Centre for English in Education at Sheffield Hallam University.

Maggie Lovatt, Key Stage 2 teacher, seconded to the Centre for English in Education.

Julia Myers, previously at Leeds Metropolitan University, now working in the Centre for English in Education.

Pete Scott, Key Stage 1 teacher, seconded to the Centre for English in Education.

Jeff Wilkinson, Senior Lecturer in Language in Education, Centre for English in Education.

The Authors

Guy Merchant coordinates the work of the Centre for English in Education at Sheffield Hallam University.

Huw Thomas is the head teacher of Springfield School, Sheffield.

'It's not as simple as that.'
J.W.

Introduction

The emphasis given to non-fiction in the National Literacy Strategy (DfEE 1998) presents a number of challenges to primary teachers. Perhaps the most significant of these challenges is the need to learn about different kinds of non-fiction texts and the terminology that can be used to explain how they work. This book provides an introduction to the classification of these text types, includes annotated examples and photocopiable activities for the classroom.

Our school system depends upon learning from the written word and using the skills of reading and writing to develop new knowledge. School children need to learn about the different ways in which texts are constructed if they are to benefit from this system. The emphasis on teaching about non-fiction in the literacy hour and in other subject areas is a way of making this learning explicit.

From the earliest stages of primary schooling, children's literacy development involves learning about *how texts work* and learning *how to make meaning* from the written word. Working effectively with these two aspects of literacy development requires sensitive teaching and the use of appropriate texts. In an earlier book, *Picture Books for the Literacy Hour* (Merchant and Thomas 1999), we emphasised the importance of the choices we make as teachers when presenting fiction to children. Here we argue that similar attention should be paid to our selection of non-fiction.

This book places its emphasis on the use of everyday texts: that is to say the sorts of non-fiction reading material that children will encounter in their social lives in home, in the wider environment, and at school. We have used a variety of sources including posters, leaflets, webpages, extracts from magazines and books as starting points for closer reading and the development of writing activities.

The first two chapters of the book introduce the reader to the importance of non-fiction and some of the terminology that is used to classify texts. The second chapter takes a critical look at the text-based approach to teaching which is sometimes referred to as *genre theory*. This chapter traces the development of this approach and its interpretation in the National Literacy Strategy (DfEE 1998). Here we include an exploration of the six text types used in the literacy hour and their linguistic characteristics.

The following chapters explore each text type in turn: *recount, report, explanation, instruction, persuasion and discussion*, providing annotated examples and suggestions for classroom activities that require a closer reading. These chapters also include starting points for writing activities and cross-curricular work. We conclude with some general guidance for teachers and schools to develop their work on non-fiction.

Chapters 3 to 8 provide practical material for use in school. These chapters have a common format which is set out in Table 1.

Table 1 Guide to Chapters 3 to 8

Features of the text type	This introduces the text type and some of its characteristic features.
Shared text	This is an example of the text type that can be used for shared work.
Annotated shared text	This shows the language features of the shared text and is intended for teacher reference.
Teacher's notes	The notes refer back to the shared text and introduce two additional sample texts and suggested classroom activities.
Sample texts	Further examples of the text type for classroom work that can be used for shared or independent work.
Activities	Photocopiable activity sheets to support a closer reading of the sample texts.
Planner	A planning sheet that children can use to think about their own non-fiction writing.

1   Range in the literacy curriculum

This chapter looks at the need for sharing a common understanding of terminology and aims to extend ideas about non-fiction text types. We begin by examining some recent influences that have shaped the way we think about literacy in school. In particular, we focus on the idea of literacy as a social practice in which different texts perform different functions. We show how this perspective influences the kind of reading and writing experiences that we provide in the classroom. This leads us to a discussion of some of the terminology we use to categorise texts, focusing specifically on the distinctions first between narrative and non-narrative, and then fiction and non-fiction. In reaching a clear view of what is meant by non-fiction, the chapter concludes with an overview of different sources of information, highlighting the diversity of non-fiction texts.

Ideas about literacy and literacy teaching

The attention given to literacy in schools in recent years has undoubtedly had a significant impact on the way that many of us think about the development of reading and writing. Not only is there increased professional confidence in the teaching of literacy, there is also a much deeper awareness of the significance of print in children's lives in and beyond the classroom. The contribution of linguists such as Halliday and Hasan (1989) and Martin (1989) enriched by the work of researchers (for example Heath 1983 and Barton and Hamilton 1998) has emphasised that literacy is essentially a *social practice*. In other words, literacy fulfils quite specific purposes in our everyday actions and interactions. Futhermore, it has been shown that the texts we read and write, as well as the ways in which we read and write them, are to a greater or lesser extent rule-bound (Halliday and Hasan 1989, Derewianka 1991).

Acknowledging the ways in which we, as adults, read and write different texts in different situations can have a powerful influence on our thoughts about literacy and literacy teaching. Our experience of texts gives us insight into the purpose that a particular text fulfils and the kind of reading it requires. So we don't look for imaginative prose and lengthy sentences with carefully chosen descriptive adjectives in the handbook for the microwave oven any more than we expect that our reading of the latest best-selling novel will help us to assemble flat-packed furniture.

If we read and write different texts in different ways and if a defining characteristic of literacy is its social nature – this must inevitably influence how we approach literacy teaching in school. Logically there are three possibilities. Firstly, we might believe that there is some way in which we could teach a basic set of literacy skills, the 'raw material' of letters, words, and sentences that children would learn to combine and use at a later date. Secondly, we could decide to construct a broad curriculum that presents a variety of opportunities for reading and writing for different purposes: a curriculum that imitates at least some of the social actions and interactions of the world at large. Thirdly, we could decide to identify a set of useful, commonly encountered types of text and explicitly teach their characteristics.

The first of these three positions, which for ease of reference we could call a basic skills approach, is the least popular for a number of reasons. The idea that the child must wait, and wait perhaps for a long time until he or she can produce or enjoy anything like a 'real' text seems to remove the intrinsic motivation that is a central feature of communication. It is interesting to note in passing that this form of 'delayed gratification' in reading and writing is still a feature of some remedial programmes. Much of what we know about young literacy learners suggests that children are already very knowledgeable about the uses of literacy when they start school (Hall 1987, Teale and Sulzby 1986). Recognising and building on this knowledge to develop reading and writing makes good sense.

The second position, based on the idea of a broad curriculum in which literacy is central, has influenced classroom practice for a number of years. This cross-curricular approach has the advantage of providing a real context for developing reading and writing which for some outweighs the difficulties of planning for a breadth of experience and progression in learning. Despite an emphasis in the National Curriculum on discrete subjects, until relatively recently, many primary schools have promoted a cross-curricular approach to literacy, particularly, as Wray and Lewis (1997) observe, in their approach to non-fiction. The opinion that this sort of approach was not particularly helpful in the drive to raise standards of literacy in schools informed the development of the National Literacy Strategy (DfEE 1998).

The third position holds that children can be explicitly taught about the features of certain text types and that this will contribute to their ability to understand what they read and to produce more effective texts of their own. This genre-based approach has been widely disseminated through the work of the Education Department of Western Australia (1997) in the *First Steps* programme and has subsequently informed the National Literacy Strategy's emphasis on teaching different text types. The terms genre and text type are used interchangeably in this book.

Re-thinking the role of narrative

Traditionally, narrative texts have enjoyed pride of place in the primary curriculum as vehicles for promoting both reading and writing development. The importance of story in early reading development is a recurrent theme in the literature (see for instance Meek 1988, Godwin and Perkins 1998, Merchant and Thomas 1999). Story entertains, it draws on the imagination and has a predictable sequential structure. These, and other features of narrative, have been used to illustrate how supportive story reading can be to the beginning reader. Partly as a result of this, professional enthusiasm for story has extended beyond the classroom: most home–school reading partnerships seek to promote the enjoyment of narrative through the use of picture books or story sacks that aim to encourage the beneficial routines observed in sharing bedtime stories (for example Taylor 1999). Although schools and teachers are beginning to recognise the importance of non-narrative reading, narrative is still dominant in many classrooms and in many teachers' minds.

In a similar fashion, practice in early writing has often tended to favour narrative forms either as the result of an emphasis on self-expression through creative writing or by encouraging children to produce recounts from first hand experience. However, critics have observed that most young children are unlikely to observe adults engaged in these kinds of writing and so have little to model their first attempts on. Most adults don't spend a lot of time on sustained writing and only a small number of those who do will be involved in creative writing. Advocates of emergent writing argue that young children develop their writing through imitating the sort of literacy practices they observe in real life situations. What has been described by Roskos and Christie (2001) as the 'play–literacy interface' in which literacy is encouraged and incorporated into socio-dramatic play based on familiar everyday situations (such as supermarkets, banks and medical centres) not only embodies a view of reading and writing as a social practice but also turns our attention to the significance of non-narrative forms in the lives of children.

Recent changes to the English Curriculum (DfEE 2000) in line with the curriculum framework of the National Literacy Strategy (DfEE 1998) prescribe the use of a range of text types in the classroom. The balance between narrative and non-narrative forms should no longer be an issue as teachers and children begin to pay closer attention to non-fiction. This development in no way undermines the role of narrative but seeks to extend and enrich children's experience of literacy.

Two kinds of narrative

Narratives are stories or accounts of events. The term narrative is often used as an alternative to 'story' or 'fiction', but at this point it is worth taking a closer look at these seemingly interchangeable terms. The story of what happened to us when we took the wrong turning on a journey or the story of a politician's misdemeanours may or may not be fictitious. Both can be told as a narrative and will have common features in terms of a concern with people, places and events and both will convey a time sequence or chronology. So the narrative form can deal with both real and imagined events. A historical narrative that covers the factual events of the Civil War and Oliver Cromwell's rise to power can be distinguished from a historical fiction in which aspects of Cromwell's character might be developed, motives explored through imagined thoughts and dialogue which is no more and no less than a product of the author's creative reconstruction of events. In her exploration of narrative, Rimmon-Kenan suggests the category description of:

> *non-fictional verbal narratives* [own emphasis] like gossip, legal testimony, news reports, history books, autobiography, personal letters etc.
>
> (Rimmon-Kenan 1983, p. 3)

Figure 1.1 shows the possible relationships between fiction, non-fiction, narrative and non-narrative forms giving examples in each category.

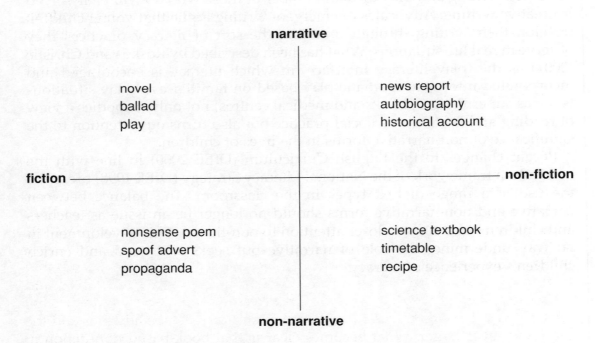

Figure 1.1 Intersections of fiction and narrative

Fact and fiction

Fiction and non-fiction have sometimes been described as artificial categories created by librarians. We learn so much about the world, people, situations, and events through fiction that the idea that this has nothing to do with fact is clearly misleading. Conversely we know that we cannot take all factual information on face value. Sources of information can be misleading or simply wrong and there are plenty of examples from all subject areas and many walks of life where such sources have been discredited as 'pure fiction'.

An important part of becoming a critical reader is developing the ability to question and check the reliability of our sources. The need for this sort of criticality is essential in an environment in which the 'information explosion' generated by electronic communication, sophisticated media manipulation through advertising and the dangers of bias and propaganda are facts of life.

We could perhaps suggest that non-fiction aims to instruct us, to provide facts or information about the real world. The reader, and of course the writer, has a certain responsibility to check these facts, but we need to begin with the assumption that we are being told the truth. Non-fiction deals with the world as it is and does not depend upon imaginary characters or events to create an imagined world. This, then, is the difference between historical fiction (such as the story *The Cellar Lad* by Theresa Tomlinson 1997) and historical information on the spread of the plague or a story in a real geographical setting (*Handa's Surprise* by Eileen Browne 1995) and a geographical text (*Postcards from Kenya* by H. Arnold 1996). While both history texts provide us with information about the Great Plague and both geography texts tell us about Kenya, the fictional accounts depend on narrative imagination (what might have happened) while the non-fiction books restrict themselves to fact (what actually happened) and the interpretation of facts.

Sources of information

If we define non-fiction as those texts which aim to instruct us and to provide facts or information about the real world we are clearly talking about a wide range of material. Environmental print in the form of signs, notices and labels perform quite basic, yet crucially important, functions in conveying information. Hoardings, posters and advertisements are also a common feature of many urban environments. Whereas catalogues, timetables and leaflets are regularly used in daily life. Newer media such as television, teletext and IT sources, including the internet, must also be added – and the list grows ever larger. What becomes clear is that book-based non-fiction in the form of textbooks, encyclopaedias and directories only account for a small portion of possible information sources. Learning about the variety of texts and the ways that they work in our complex society is a crucial aspect of literacy development.

In the chapters that follow we will be exploring the language features of the more common non-fiction text types, drawing our examples from real-life texts. These examples will be used to demonstrate how we can teach primary-age children how to interpret non-fiction and how to experiment with and develop their own writing.

Conclusion

This chapter has drawn attention to the range of reading and writing that is an essential part of the primary curriculum. We have explored the implications of understanding literacy as a social practice and looked at some of the everyday terminology we use to describe texts. This has included clarification of the distinctions between narrative and non-narrative, and fiction and non-fiction. We have suggested a working definition of non-fiction and shown the diversity of forms which that category includes. In summary:

- **Literacy is a social practice.**
- **Genres are socially recognised kinds of texts.**
- **There are differences between narrative and non-narrative genres.**
- **Genres conveying factual information are described as non-fiction.**
- **Non-fiction includes a wide range of information sources.**

2 Classifying text types

This chapter looks at ways of classifying non-fiction texts. We begin by giving an overview of the development of genre theory and its classroom applications. After examining some of the criticisms of genre theory we move on to an exploration of how this work has been used to inform curriculum guidance including the *First Steps* programme and the non-fiction strand of the National Literacy Strategy. This leads into an exploration of the six text types commonly used in the literacy hour. We then discuss some of the issues raised when we try to classify texts, focusing particularly on variation within genres. The last section returns to the genre debate and outlines how a focus on text types can be used as a starting point for developing critical literacy.

Genre theory

In order to make sense of the current emphasis on text types in the curriculum it is useful to begin by exploring the area of genre theory. As we have seen, some of the most influential work in this area was done in Australia in the 1980s by Kress (1982), Martin (1989) and Halliday and Hasan (1989) who were exploring the applications of a functional approach to language – that is to say, an approach which emphasises how language, both written and spoken, enables us to *do* things in different social contexts. Their work showed how texts fulfil socially determined goals and have distinctive linguistic patterns. These patterns are the choices we make in terms of textual organisation, grammatical structure and vocabulary when, for example, we write out a recipe, an explanatory letter or a poster; language choices which are further modified to indicate the relationship between reader and writer (such as the degree of formality or intimacy).

Genres then are socially accepted ways of using language. They are not determined by hard and fast rules; they allow for considerable variation and can, of course, change or evolve. Letter writing can be used to illustrate these points. Apart from the basic requirement that a letter needs to identify who it is addressed *to* and normally signals who it is *from*, we can anticipate considerable variation depending on the level of formality, the relationship between the writer and the reader, the purpose for writing and the topic. Although there are certain conventions of layout, ways of opening and closing and so on, we do have choices to make. As well as this we will also be aware that these conventions change over time – just like other forms of language. So the ways in which we were first taught to layout letters may well have subsequently changed. Decisions about where to place the sender's address, how to punctuate the address, forms of salutation and closure are all subject to variation and change. Newer communication media also generate new forms. E-mails and faxes, although similar in many ways to the letter, have a distinctive appearance and are beginning to develop their own generic language features.

The use of genre theory in exploring classroom texts has been further developed in Australia (Christie 1989, Derewianka 1991, Wing Jan 1991) and in the UK (Littlefair 1991, Wray and Lewis 1997). Looking at genres can help us to audit the range of reading and writing in different curriculum areas, to analyse the different texts provided as a resource in schools and classrooms and to develop teaching approaches which explicitly focus on the language features needed to help children to read and write different text types.

Criticisms of genre theory

Genre theory is not without its critics – particularly when the pedagogical implications are considered. Perhaps the most significant criticism alerts us to the fact that a genre-based school curriculum *could* encourage a teacher-directed 'transmission' model which over-emphasises specific language features associated with a narrow range of genres. Czerniewska (1992), describing this as 'genre orthodoxy', suggests that:

> What is worrying is if categorical statements are made about what genres are acceptable and what are not or about the major genres necessary for all children to learn in order to meet society's writing demands. The danger is that such judgements can be turned into a writing policy whereby each child practices the required genre until an agreed stage of proficiency is reached.
>
> (Czerniewska 1992, p. 149)

Recent developments in the National Literacy Strategy (DfEE 2000, DfEE 2001) remind us that this sort of approach is always a possibility if we are not clear about our reasons for teaching about text types and the teaching principles which we apply.

Curriculum designers who embrace genre theory are faced with difficult decisions in identifying which text types are important, where in the curriculum they should be studied and at what stage. The *First Steps* approach (Education Department of Western Australia 1997) is based on a model for promoting successful writing in the school context. So the emphasis is on existing school genres which are found in different subject areas of the curriculum. This may help children to access the curriculum through, for example, learning how to write an essay (exposition), but does it help them to understand and critique text in the wider social environment?

Other critics of genre theory maintain that the emphasis given to texts and textual features leads us to overlook the developmental needs of young writers.

Barrs (1994) argues for a recognition of the generic features of children's writing which are different from the genres identified by linguists, whereas followers of Graves' (1983) school of 'process writing' worry that young writers will not find their own voice and that the complexities of the compositional process will be simplified as children are increasingly encouraged to model their writing on existing texts.

Clearly it is important to keep a balanced view when looking at genre-based teaching. We need to be able to encourage reading and writing that has a real purpose with content that is relevant or significant to the literacy learner. In other words we must not forget the importance of *context* in our endeavours to teach about text:

> the generic characteristics of any given text, whilst being linguistically complex, are less powerful determinants of children's literacy development than social interactions around those texts, during reading and writing.
>
> (Webster *et al*. 1996, p. 24)

First Steps and the National Literacy Strategy

As we saw in the first chapter the influential work of the *First Steps* programme (Education Department of Western Australia 1997) develops genre theory into curriculum guidance for primary-age pupils. In the introductory chapters to the writing strand of the above work the authors acknowledge the ways in which different theories inform their approach. They claim that genre theory provides the emphasis given to developing writers' awareness of different texts and registers, asserting that:

> the forms of writing selected . . . are generally considered to be those often required in primary and secondary settings.
>
> (Education Department of Western Australia 1997, p. 19)

The *First Steps* programme identifies six 'forms of writing' that are in effect school-based genres. These are shown below with the purposes described by the authors of the programme:

- Narratives (with a purpose to entertain).
- Recounts (with a purpose to retell events).
- Procedures (with a purpose to describe the way we do things).
- Reports (with a purpose to classify and describe things).
- Explanations (with a purpose to explain phenomena).
- Expositions (with a purpose to argue and persuade).

In contrast, *The National Literacy Strategy Framework for Teaching* (DfEE 1998) does not articulate the theoretical basis of its curriculum guidelines[1] but does provide a breakdown which shows a sequential approach to the coverage of

---

[1] The influence of Australian genre theorists as well as others on the non-fiction strand of the National Literacy Strategy have subsequently been acknowledged (see Beard 1998, pp. 47–8).

fiction (including poetry) and non-fiction in the primary years. This summary of 'range' details quite specific kinds of texts (for example, labels, letters, instructions, dictionaries and information texts) although these are not grouped according to their generic characteristics. It is only in the training support material that the concept of genre or 'text type' is introduced – and then only in the context of non-fiction.

The six text types

Following a similar line of argument to that of the authors of the *First Steps* programme, Lewis and Wray (1995) identify six text types that are common school-based genres. These are described as 'the main types of non-fiction writing' (Wray and Lewis 1997, p. 118). Lewis and Wray's (1995) classification, subsequently adopted by the National Literacy Strategy, is slightly different from the *First Steps* model. This is shown in Figure 2.1.

Text type	Purpose
recount	retelling events for information or entertainment
report	describing the way things are
explanation	explaining processes (natural or social); how things work
procedure*	describing how things are done (in sequence)
persuasive	promoting a point of view or argument
discussion	presenting different viewpoints

* Procedural texts are sometimes referred to as *instructions* in the NLS material.

Figure 2.1 The six text types used in the National Literacy Strategy (adapted from Wray and Lewis 1997)

The differences between the two lists of text types are as follows. The *First Steps* model includes *narrative* (fiction) whereas the National Literacy Strategy restricts itself to non-fiction. Texts that aim to argue or persuade are shown as two distinct types by the National Literacy Strategy (*persuasion* and *discussion*) whereas they are grouped together as *exposition* in the *First Steps* programme.

Identifying text types

As we have seen, the six text types are classified according to their purpose, but it is important to remember that there is considerable variation within each category. So while we are able to identify *common* linguistic features these are not necessarily *essential* features of the genre. This is a result of the fact that writers, consciously or unconsciously, adapt the language (or register) they use for particular effect. One such influence concerns the relationship between the writer and the reader. This may affect layout, the level of detail required, the grammatical complexity and the choice of vocabulary. For example, an explanatory text about changing states of matter designed for eight year olds will differ considerably from one aimed at undergraduates. The instructions for operating the burglar alarm you leave for a friend who is staying in your house will look very different from those in the manual which will be far more detailed and addressed to a wider (unknown) audience.

The language of a particular genre is also, of course, influenced by the subject content. This is easiest to see when we consider textbooks for different curriculum areas in which particular topics are associated with technical vocabulary. For example, in science, terms like attraction, repulsion and polarity constitute the technical vocabulary of magnetism and everyday words like weight, force and pressure take on more specialised meanings. Subject content has an affect on all texts. Think of the ways in which the language of a personal letter may vary according to the issues discussed or an advertisement according to the product it promotes.

Asking some quite basic questions about the texts you choose can be a useful way in to looking at and classifying texts. The list that follows can be used as a starting point.

- **Who wrote the text?** (is it a single author; is the author named; are they writing in a personal or official capacity?)
- **What was their reason for writing it?** (do they hope you will understand, enjoy, be persuaded, act, buy, etc.?)
- **Who do they hope will read it?** (is it written for an individual; a particular group or a wider audience?)
- **What is the relationship between writer and reader?** (friend to friend; expert to learner; official authority to public, etc.).

In studying everyday texts, similar questions can be used with children to begin to develop an understanding of how texts work and the sort of choices that writers make. This approach will help in appreciating the fact that text types are variable and not governed by immutable rules.

Figure 2.2 provides more detail about the six text types referred to in the National Literacy Strategy (DfEE 1998). It shows some common linguistic features of each genre at text, sentence and word level which are applicable to text types from the school curriculum as well as from other contexts. The texts you use, and the texts that children write may or may not include these features. Remember that the language features that are chosen reflect the issues and questions referred to in this section. The 'Quick guide to the terminology' in Figure 2.2 provides a brief gloss on technical terms used to describe text types. Perhaps it is worth emphasising at this point, that these terms are not exclusively tied to specific text types; neither are they the only way of describing linguistic features.

	Text	Sentence	Word
Recount *Diary, autobiography, news report.*	Reconstruction of past experience – actions and events involving real people are described. These are organised in chronological sequence. May have a simple story structure and a title that attracts the reader's attention.	Usually told in the past (narrative) tense with adverbial clauses and temporal connectives. In a news recount careful thought is given to the headline sentence.	Specific locations (proper nouns), names and personal pronouns. Will tend to use verbs of action.
Report *Encyclopaedia, information leaflet or poster.*	Hierarchical organisation: a general category (e.g. volcanoes) followed by types (e.g. active, dormant) describing parts or characteristics. Non-chronological organisation. May include diagrams.	Often written in the simple present tense. Uses topic sentences to orientate the reader (e.g. there are three types of volcano).	Generic participants and locations. Technical or subject-specific vocabulary. Verbs performing an existential or relational function.
Explanation *Textbook explaining scientific phenomena, explanatory letter.*	Logical progression of statements which explain a process or sequence of events. Often begin by stating the phenomenon or by asking a question. May include diagrams.	Often written in the simple present tense using temporal or causal connectives. May include passive sentences.	Generic participants and locations. Verbs describing actions and processes. Technical or subject-specific vocabulary.
Instruction *Recipe, manual instructions for a game.*	Usually organised in chronological sequence detailing a number of stages. May include lists of materials, numbered sentences and diagrams. States the goal, the materials and the method.	Imperative sentences including adverbial clauses and temporal (and causal) connectives. Often make use of simple sentences.	Generic participants and locations although the reader may be directly addressed through the use of personal pronouns.
Persuasion *Public information poster, advertising leaflet, magazine article.*	Often include a slogan or short sentence that highlights the topic or product. The opening statement is often followed by a justification of point of view, issue or product. May have a problem-solution pattern. Makes careful use of visual images and layout.	Often uses simple, catchy sentences (or word play) to state a fact or opinion. May make some use of imperative sentences. Causal connectives will be used in the justification.	Usually written in the simple present tense. May refer to whole classes of objects (e.g. wildlife) or specific proper nouns (e.g brand names). May increase a sense of interaction with the use of personal pronouns ('we' and 'you').
Discussion *Essays, some newspaper articles.*	Begins with the statement of a contentious issue. Two sides of the debate are presented with supporting evidence, ending with questions or conclusions. May make use of subheadings.	Uses topic sentences to orientate the reader. Will use a variety of cohesive devices including logical, additional and oppositional connectives. Use of passive sentences.	Usually written in the simple present tense referring to generic participants (human or non-human) or abstract issues, ideas or opinions. Likely to include subject-specific terminology.

Figure 2.2 The linguistic features of the six text types

> ## *Quick guide to the terminology used in Figure 2.2*
>
> **additional connectives** – connectives that indicate additional information (e.g. 'also'; 'furthermore')
>
> **adverbial clauses** – clauses of time, place or manner (e.g. 'after a few days'; 'by the side of an old farmhouse')
>
> **causal connectives** – connectives indicating cause and effect (e.g. 'as a result'; 'so'; 'because')
>
> **chronological sequence** – texts in which there is a clear sense of the order of events
>
> **existential function** – verbs that indicate that something exists (e.g. 'is'; 'are'; 'exists')
>
> **generic participants** – nouns that refer to a group of objects (e.g. 'plants' or 'buildings')
>
> **logical connectives** – connectives used to develop an argument (e.g. 'the reason for this'; 'therefore'; 'because of')
>
> **non-chronological organisation** – texts which do not describe a sequence of events (e.g. text organised according to topic or listed in alphabetical order)
>
> **imperative sentences** – sentences used to instruct or direct beginning with a verb (e.g. '*Squeeze* the glue onto the cardboard'; '*Align* the two sections', in which verbs are underlined)
>
> **oppositional connectives** – connectives that indicate contrast (e.g. 'however'; 'nevertheless'; 'on the other hand')
>
> **passive sentences** – sentences in which the subject is passive (e.g. 'the rocks are worn away by the action of water'; or 'the rocks are worn away' in which 'rocks' is the subject)
>
> **personal pronouns** – words used to refer to specific participants (e.g. 'I/me'; 'she/him'; 'they/them')
>
> **proper nouns** – names of people, places, organisations, etc.
>
> **relational function** – verbs that relate one part of a statement to another (e.g. ' Finches *belong to* a group of birds . . . '; 'They *are* small seed-eating . . . ')
>
> **story structure** – overall pattern of a story (e.g. orientation, problem, solution, ending)
>
> **temporal connectives** – connectives indicating the passage of time (e.g. 'meanwhile', 'later', 'afterwards')
>
> **topic sentences** – sentences which act as signposts to the reader introducing a particular topic (usually found at the beginning of paragraphs)

Finding good examples of the six text types to use in the classroom can be quite difficult. Texts are not always easy to classify. The descriptions used in the following chapters, which focus on text, sentence and word level features of each type, will be a useful guide. But, as we observed earlier in this chapter, although genres can be described as socially recognised ways of using language, they are not determined by hard and fast rules.

You will find that there are, in fact, more non-fiction genres than those listed above and those covered in this book. There are also forms of writing that can fit several genre categories (see Figure 2.3) and many examples of mixed genre texts. As Derewianka (1991) comments in the conclusion to her book:

> When you start looking closely at texts...you will find that not all texts have such a readily recognised schematic structure...out in the real world you might come across texts which differ somewhat from the descriptions offered here.
>
> (Derewianka 1991, p. 82)

Purpose	Participants
To persuade	Mail order company writing to potential customers on a database
To inform	Head teacher writing to parents about a forthcoming school event
To recount	Close relative or friend writing a personal letter about recent news
To explain	Insurance company writing to client about the process of agreeing a claim

Figure 2.3 Purposes and participants in letter writing

Critical literacy

Earlier in this chapter we looked at the professional debate about genre theory. We can see two main trends in this debate. Firstly, there are those (like Martin 1989) who argue that helping children to understand the characteristics of different kinds of writing enables them to access the whole curriculum. Secondly, there are those who argue that genre-based teaching may actually constrain children by exposing them to a narrow range of writing and result in teacher-led 'transmission' of text types (Czerniewska 1992). We are of the opinion that careful and critical examination of text types is a central concern of literacy teaching. An important resource for this sort of work are the texts that children encounter in their everyday life – texts that are situated in the context of their social lives. Beginning with these everyday texts provides opportunities for encouraging children to see how texts work, how they represent the world and how they position the reader. In this way we see the exploration of text types as the starting point for 'critical literacy' (Christie and Misson 1998). However, simplifying the study of texts is a practice that comes with a health warning. Contrived and specifically prepared materials demonstrating the features and stimulating the production of text types have limited uses – something we acknowledge in this text and has been stated by other writers (Lewis and Wray 1997). An understanding of text types is a starting point, not a goal in itself.

Conclusion

Recognising that language and literacy are social practices leads us to an understanding of the patterned nature of texts. We saw in Chapter 1 how texts can be grouped into types or genres according to their purpose. Developing a typology for non-fiction text types is a complex undertaking and raises important issues when we consider the literacy curriculum. In this chapter we have looked at the professional debate raised by genre theory and traced its influence on curriculum documents. We have concluded by showing how an awareness of genre can be seen as the starting point for developing a critical literacy. In summary:

- **Genres are not fixed – there is considerable variation.**
- **Classroom applications of genre theory have been controversial.**
- **Curriculum documents tend to focus on school-based genres.**
- **Texts that children experience in different contexts can be used.**
- **The six text types can be used to describe a wider variety of texts.**
- **Understanding of genre can be a starting point for critical literacy.**

3 Recount

FEATURES OF TEXT TYPE

Recounts tell the story of events, usually in the order that they actually occurred. 'Real life' narratives may include reference to people, their actions and the places in which these are set. Some typical features of the recount genre are shown below.

	Text	Sentence	Word
Recount *E.g.: biography, news report, some diaries or journals.*	• reconstruction of past experience • actions and events involving real life narratives • organised in chronological sequence • simple story structure • title that attracts the reader's attention	• past (narrative) tense • adverbial clauses • temporal connectives • catchy headlines • short paragraphs	• specific locations (proper nouns) • names and personal pronouns • verbs of action

Quick guide to terminology

adverbial clauses – clauses of time, place or manner (e.g. 'after a few days', 'by the side of an old farmhouse')

chronological sequence – texts in which there is a clear sense of the order of events

personal pronouns – words used to refer to specific participants (e.g. 'I/me'; 'she/him'; 'they/them'

story structure – overall pattern of a story (e.g. orientation, problem, solution, ending)

proper nouns – names of people, places, organisations, etc.

temporal connectives – connectives indicating the passage of time (e.g. 'meanwhile', 'later', 'afterwards')

SHARED TEXT

Recount: Diary entry

June 12th

Today I had a bit of a disaster. Early this morning we were at school. During the morning my Football key ring fell out of my pocket and Mr Crow grabbed it. He put it on his desk. I was really upset because it is so special.

While we were supposed to be working Shaun said he reckoned we could swipe the key ring back. Then he said we should stay behind in the classroom when everybody went out and swipe it off the desk. I wasn't sure, but I really wanted the key ring back.

Later on, at playtime we hid under the tables when everyone went out. The problem was old Crow locked the classroom door, so we missed playtime.

After school, Crow gave the key ring back and said if he saw it again he would have me 'sent off'. He thinks he's really funny.

ANNOTATED SHARED TEXT

reconstruction of past experience	June 12th Today I had a bit of a disaster. Early this morning we were at school. During the morning my Football key ring fell out of my pocket and Mr Crow grabbed it. He put it on his desk. I was really upset because it is so special.	past (narrative) tense specific locations e.g. 'school'
actions and events involving real people	While we were supposed to be working Shaun said he reckoned we could swipe the key ring back. Then he said we should stay behind in the classroom when everybody went out and swipe it off the desk. I wasn't sure, but I really wanted the key ring back.	names and personal pronouns, e.g. 'Mr Crow' short paragraphs
organised in chronological sequence	Later on, at playtime we hid under the tables when everyone went out. The problem was old Crow locked the classroom door, so we missed playtime.	temporal connectives, e.g. 'then', 'later' verbs of action, e.g. 'locked', 'hid'
simple story structure	After school, Crow gave the key ring back and said if he saw it again he would have me 'sent off'. He thinks he's really funny.	adverbial clauses

TEACHER'S NOTES

Shared Recount Text: Diary entry

The diary entry is rooted in the sort of experience children might feel has personal relevance, a diary of events at school. The structure follows a chronological order but it is worth pointing out that the writer has selected one incident from the school day. Children could discuss why this is the case.

The chronological organisation is structured around clear paragraphs. These provide a vital way into reading and writing of longer recounts. As a scene changes or as time moves on a new paragraph is taken. They act a bit like a scene change in a film, giving the reader a clear indication that the text has moved on. One way of exploring this is to ask children to provide subtitles for paragraphs in a recount, so in this example they might entitle the opening paragraph: 'Crow grabs key ring'.

Point out the specific language used. Names and places are clear. Verb choice is also important: Mr Crow didn't pick up the key ring. He 'grabbed' it. The children planned to 'swipe' it back.

SAMPLE TEXTS

Sample Text A: Does the Beast of Bodmin exist?

Like the diary entry this is a recount from a child. It forms a piece of evidence surrounding a disputed fact: the existence of a beast on Bodmin Moor. Like the Loch Ness monster or other pieces of folklore, such tales thrive on disputed recounts.

Point out the title, raising the question. How might a text like this answer a question?

Ask children to list the details they are given in the text. It is more than just a statement of 'I once saw a big creature by a bus'. Details are vital to improving the writing of recounts.

Sample Text B: Mary Seacole

Biography and autobiography are two common forms of factual recount. This potted biography provides the basic facts about a famous heroine.

Work through some of the facts presented in the recount:

- birth details – point out the dates at the top
- what the famous person did – this will generate a list of actions but often famous people are remembered for one clear activity by which they made their mark
- how others reacted to them – the opinions of contemporaries
- why they are remembered – what significance do figures from the past have for us today?

The latter two are particularly important. Unrecognised characters from the past have proved enduring in history. Controversial figures abound in history projects, such as the Tudors and the Victorians.

ACTIVITIES

Photocopiable 1

'What happened?'. Given the disputable nature of the story told in Sample Text A, this activity looks at the whole process of grilling the author or teller of a recount. In research, oral history and factual reportage, such questions gather in the facts that form the basis of a recount. Children might like to follow this activity by creating their own questions and answers for the child recounting the diary entry in the Shared Text.

Photocopiable 2

'Biography details'. This activity transfers the features of a biography, noted in the Mary Seacole text, into an opportunity for children to locate similar information about other famous people. These may be researched from the internet or library texts. Having filled in the grid, children can then try to create their own brief biography of the person they have researched. One way of approaching this is to ask them to recount that life but to place a limit on the number of words they can use, as would have been the case with the Mary Seacole article. What events will they major on? How will they précis longer sections of a life story?

Photocopiable 3

'Recount facts'. Factual details are a vital part of a recount text. In this activity children confront a range of statements about Mary Seacole. As they sort true from false there will be a number of disputed statements. These include those where the text does not state a fact but children might infer it from the text, such as 'Mary wanted to be a doctor when she was very young'. The question is whether such inferences can be supported by the text.

Writing

Writing a recount text can involve personal experience or researched events.

- Pointers for writing include the need to pick apart an event into a series of constituent elements. In the diary entry one story is planned over a series of events. The splitting and structuring of events keeps children from making cursory references to events in their writing. The diary entry could have been 'I got in trouble 'cos I dropped my key ring and ended up locked in the classroom', but instead the events have been planned.
- Paragraphing provides a useful means of structuring the presentation of events over time.

- Details can be listed and can act as a useful planning tool, often providing a time structure as with dates in a life story.
- Dialogue provides an insight into an event from the point of view of those who were there. Through dialogue we encounter the expressions of those on the scene. In recounting past events the writer sometimes needs to embellish a conversation by filling out an exchange that might have occurred between two people. We don't have access to Mary Seacole's conversation with the War Office but could develop one for a reconstruction of these events.
- Thoughts and feelings give an insight into how it was to be a part of an event. A good recount can place us inside the shoes of those who were party to events.

PLANNER

Photocopiable Planner

One event is unpacked in a way that pulls out the details of the text. See page 30.

Does the Beast of Bodmin exist?

I was on a school trip to Bodicote near Banbury, on Thursday 23 March, from Kingham Primary School in Oxfordshire. On the way back to school, at about 12.40, I spotted from the coach a large black cat in a field, near some sheep. We were about 15 to 20 minutes from Bodicote. The cat was walking very slowly and the sheep ran away. I could make out that it was a big black cat as it was quite close to the bus. I think it was a panther or a jaguar. I saw the NEWSROUND article on big cats today and thought I would write.

Joshua, Kingham Primary School

From *In the News* 25/5/01, BBC Education

Mary Seacole

Mary Seacole cared for soldiers in the Crimean War. She was born in Kingston, Jamaica, to a Scottish army officer father and a Jamaican mother, and learned how to mix herbal medicines and treat yellow fever and cholera when she was young.

She called herself a 'doctress' and took her skills to England. But the War Office refused her offer of help during the Crimean War so she set off at her own expense, as a sutler, a supplier of food and drink. She opened a canteen, known as the British Hotel, near the battlefield of Balaclava. Carrying a basket of food, bandages and medicines she could be seen on the battlefield helping the wounded.

She became so well known among the soldiers that she was noticed by William Russell, of *The Times* newspaper. He organised a fund when she returned home – a popular heroine but destitute. She wrote a book, *The Wonderful Adventures of Mrs Seacole in Many Lands*, but her fame did not last. Her story was rediscovered and the book was reprinted in 1984.

From *Junior Education* (April 2000)

What happened?

Here are some questions readers of this recount might have.

How would the writer answer?

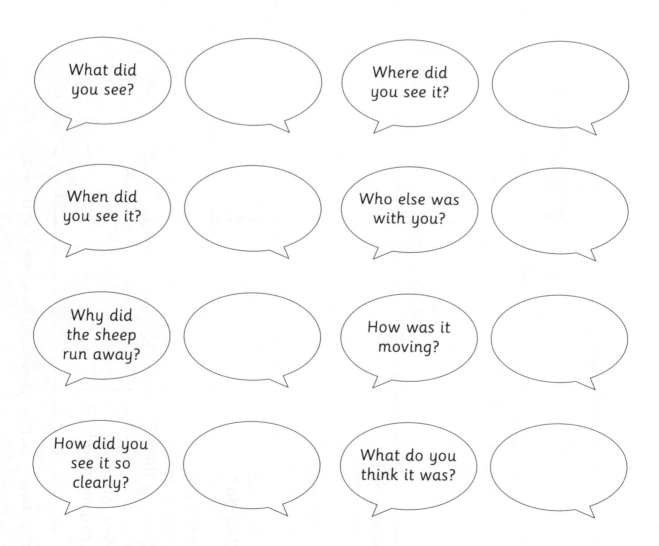

What did
you see?

Where did
you see it?

When did
you see it?

Who else was
with you?

Why did
the sheep
run away?

How was it
moving?

How did you
see it so
clearly?

What do you
think it was?

Biography details

Fill in the biography details for Mary Seacole and three other famous people. Use library books or encyclopaedias to help you.

	Mary Seacole			
Where were they born?				
When were they born?				
What did they do?				
What did other people think of them?				
Why are they memorable?				

Recount facts

Here are some sentences about Mary Seacole.
Cut them out and sort them into
True, False and Not Sure

Mary Seacole cared for sailors in the Second World War	Mary raised money for the Crimean soldiers	The soldiers thought Mary was wonderful
William Russell told people about Mary Seacole	Mary's book was forgotten for a long time	Mary wanted to be a doctor when she was very young
Mary walked across dangerous battlefields	Mary became very rich and famous	Mary came to England offering to help in Crimea
Mary's father was a doctor	Mary Seacole spent all she had getting to Balaclava	The War Office asked Mary to help in Crimea

© Guy Merchant and Huw Thomas (2001) *Non-Fiction for the Literacy Hour*

Recount details

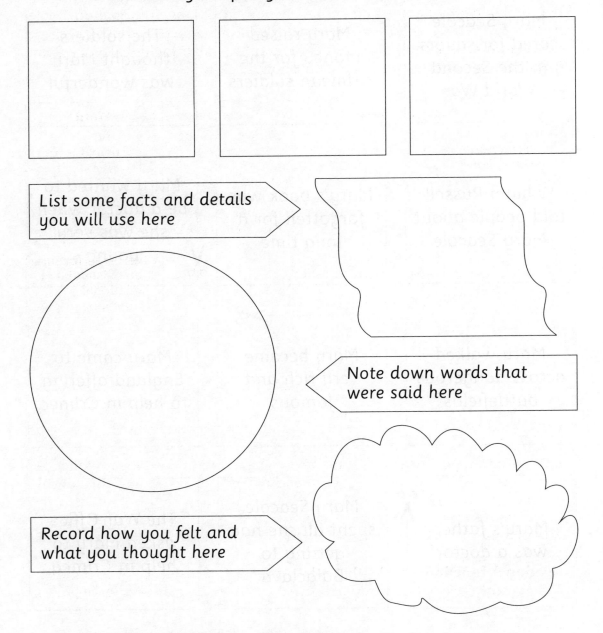

What is your recount about?

How will you split your recount into 3 events?

List some facts and details you will use here

Note down words that were said here

Record how you felt and what you thought here

4 Report

FEATURES OF TEXT TYPE

Reports are texts that provide information about animate or inanimate objects. Their function is to classify and define phenomena. Many 'information' books for primary school children – particularly those aimed at developing an understanding of natural science and geography – fall into this category. Some typical features of the report genre are shown below.

	Text	Sentence	Word
Report *E.g.: encyclopaedia, information leaflet, poster.*	• hierarchical organisation • general category (e.g. volcanoes) followed by types (e.g. active, dormant) describing parts/characteristics • non-chronological organisation • may use diagrams	• simple present tense • topic sentences to orientate the reader (e.g. there are three types of volcano)	• generic participants and locations • technical or subject-specific vocabulary • verbs performing an existential or relational function

---

Quick guide to terminology

existential function – verbs that indicate that something exists (e.g. 'is'; 'are'; 'exists')

non-chronological organisation – texts which do not describe a sequence of events (e.g. text organised according to topic or listed in alphabetical order)

topic sentences – sentences which act as signposts to the reader introducing a particular topic (usually found at the beginning of paragraphs)

relational function – verbs that relate one part of a statement to another (e.g. 'Finches *belong to* a group of birds...'; 'They *are* small seed-eating...')

SHARED TEXT

Report: Five pillars

Islam is one of the world's major religions and its believers are called Muslims. In Islam there are five pillars. These are five important beliefs that every Muslim must follow.

The first of these, Tahweed, is the pillar of believing the teaching of Islam.

Salat is the practice of praying five times a day. There are five prayer times set by the passage of the sun across the earth. Muslim people wash before praying and face the holy city of Mecca to pray.

Sawm, or fasting, takes place during the time of Ramadan. There are a number of rules to be obeyed during a fast time. Muslim people do not eat or drink during day time. They also have to think carefully about their behaviour. Some people, such as women who are pregnant, do not have to fast.

Another pillar, Zakat, involves giving to those in need.

Finally, the Hajj is the pilgrimage to Mecca, the most holy place for Muslims. Muslims are expected to take this journey at least once in their lifetime.

Together these five pillars are the main features of the Muslim faith.

ANNOTATED SHARED TEXT

hierarchical organisation	Islam is one of the world's major religions and its believers are called Muslims. In Islam there are five pillars. These are five important beliefs that every Muslim must follow.	generic participants and locations
general category describing parts/ characteristics	The first of these, Tahweed, is the pillar of believing the teaching of Islam. Salat is the practice of praying five times a day. There are five prayer times set by the passage of the sun across the earth. Muslim people wash before praying and face the holy city of Mecca to pray.	simple present tense
non-chronological organisation	Sawm, or fasting, takes place during the time of Ramadan. There are a number of rules to be obeyed during a fast time. Muslim people do not eat or drink during day time. They also have to think carefully about their behaviour. Some people, such as women who are pregnant, do not have to fast.	topic sentences to orientate the reader (e.g. 'There are a number of rules...')
	Another pillar, Zakat, involves giving to those in need. Finally, the Hajj is the pilgrimage to Mecca, the most holy place for Muslims. Muslims are expected to take this journey at least once in their lifetime. Together these five pillars are the main features of the Muslim faith.	technical or subject-specific vocabulary verbs performing an existential or relational function, e.g. 'Hajj *is*...' and 'pillars *are*...'

TEACHER'S NOTES

Shared Report Text: Five pillars

This RE text presents the five pillars of Islam, reporting on aspects of each pillar. The text follows the pattern of a report in that, beginning with an overarching subject, it works through aspects of that one subject. Children could read the text and locate the way in which it is structured by looking at the number of sections into which they could divide the text. Having done this they could look at what each section is about.

Report texts often generalise. This is not the recount of a particular person's experience of their faith but a generic report on features of the religion. Such features apply to a number of specific participants, but the report generalises.

This is reflected in the way the report is structured. Non-chronological organisation is used, e.g. 'the Hajj is the pilgrimage...', 'Zakat, involves giving...'. Ask the question 'When?' of these statements and the answer is 'Always'. Report texts do not deal in particular instances of Hajj or Zakat. They generalise in the way they define their subject matter.

SAMPLE TEXTS

Sample Text A: Graves Park

This leaflet provides a guide to a visitors' attraction. The single location is reported through a series of paragraphs, majoring on specific themes. Children could be encouraged to provide subheadings for these.

Following an initial read of the text, children could pick out a list of separate pieces of information imparted in the report. The organisational skill in producing such a text often lies in coalescing these varied facts into clearly structured paragraphs.

Sample Text B: Earth

This section of a non-fiction book on space provides a basic report on a scientific phenomena.

As well as reporting on the Earth, this text has the interesting addition of exploring possibilities around its subject matter (e.g. 'If Earth were nearer to the sun, it would be too hot...'). Report texts can often present a range of possible states for their subject matter.

Children should be encouraged to pick out the adjectives in this text. A number of report texts will provide interesting uses of adjectives, offering a fuller description of the subject matter on which they report.

ACTIVITIES

Photocopiable 1

'Information Packing'. The paragraphing together of various facts in the Graves Park leaflet was noted above. In this activity children are encouraged to work with this idea, extending the paragraphs with new information. This should be an active task, with children cutting up copies of the leaflet and the 'Information Packing' rectangles.

Photocopiable 2

'Planet Paragraphs'. Sticking with the organisation of reports, this activity also asks children to begin with a set of notes and transfer these into cohesive paragraphs of text. Children could aim to order the facts they will refer to in their report, possibly numbering the facts listed in the notes in the order in which they will use this information.

Photocopiable 3

'Draw it – Report it'. An essential element of report writing is the ability to pick apart the features of the subject matter, getting the notes from which to write the text. This activity uses drawing as a means of encouraging children to make such notes. The idea isn't that they should draw something then do the notes, but rather to spend a bit of time drawing then noting features or facts about the subject of the picture. They can then return to drawing, then noting facts, and continuing this exchange between drawing and noting. As they do this the drawings may gain in detail – and so will the material for their report text.

Writing

Report writing involves some specific activities to prompt the collection and organisation of information.

- Fact gathering is a basic part of the report writing process. It links well to the observational aspect of science, in which children gather information about things they see.
- The splitting of the subject matter provides a basic structure for a report. There is something to be said for planning a report on a few smaller pieces of paper, gathering information about one subject on different note pages. So a report about a school could be planned with one page dedicated to the

playground, another to the hall, another to the office, etc. This split plan encourages the organisation of paragraphs that separately build up a picture of the whole subject.

• Exaggerate particularity. This may seem like an odd exercise but children can quite enjoy the wordplay involved in overdoing the precision needed in a piece of report writing! The table on which they are working may seem like any other table, but it can be the sort of subject about which they can extend the precision of their reporting, commenting on the 'metal, cylindrical legs, painted blue and ending in a plastic stopper'. This makes a good oral activity – it's not one for writing!

• Specific sentences can be analysed to see what information could have been imported into them to improve the report. If a report says 'The door is broken', there is more that can be asked: Which door? How is it broken? Where is the break? One way of developing this idea is for children to work in threes or fours, with individuals either writing statements about a subject or contributing sentences from a report text they have written. The sentence is written at the centre of a large sheet of paper. The job of the other children is to write some questions around the sentence. This can lead to a refinement of the sentence to something more like: 'The main school door is dented along the bottom'. The aim should be to refine the information so that the picture in words is improved.

• Quick reports can foster this type of writing. Provide children with an array of photos face down on the table. These should be as varied as possible: a lock, a frog, the school, a Fun Fair. Postcards can provide a good resource for this task. The children turn these up one at a time and write a brief report on what they see, e.g. 'There is a big wheel in the middle of the fair. The fair stands alongside the beach'. The reports can be short, two sentence texts, practising the features of the text type.

PLANNER

Photocopiable Planner

The basic planning pattern for a report presented here (see page 42) focuses on that task of listing information to be organised into paragraphs. It can work with the 'Draw it – Report it' task.

REPORT: SAMPLE TEXT A

Graves Park

GRAVES PARK
ANIMAL FARM

Graves Park Animal Farm provides a home to some of the rarest breeds of farm animals in the country.

The children's farmyard offers an opportunity to view a range of small and young animals at close hand. There are handling enclosures, seats and tables, a classroom, plus toilet and hand washing facilities.

School parties, informal visitors, families and other groups are made welcome at the farm every day of the year. (Please see overleaf for group booking details.)

Donations and sponsorship are gratefully received, enabling the work of the farm to be developed.

The Animal farm is continually being improved and updated, as funds allow.

Recent developments include an Owl Flight and Natural History area.

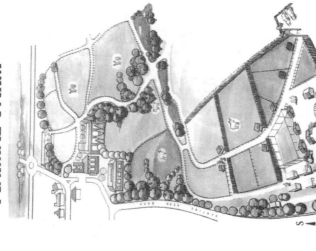

HEMSWORTH ROAD . SHEFFIELD

37

Earth

Earth is a smallish, rocky planet. It is in just the right place in the Solar System to allow **life** to be supported. If Earth were nearer to the Sun, it would be too hot for life as we know it to survive. If it were further away, it would be too cold.

Seen from Space, Earth is a beautiful **bluish disc** with swirling white clouds. It looks blue because so much of its surface is ocean.

From *1001 Facts about Space* by Pam Beasant. Published by Kingfisher Books (1992)

Information Packing

Here are some rectangles containing extra information about
Graves Park.
Cut up a copy of the GRAVES PARK ANIMAL FARM leaflet and the extra
rectangles. Slot the rectangles into the leaflet where they best fit.

Wensleydales and South
downs are among the rare
breeds of sheep on the farm

Alongside the farm animals
there are domesticated
animals, such as rabbits
and guinea pigs

One cow can eat a whole
bag of cow feed in a week,
aside from needing grass
and hay!

 A tawny owl provides a
chance to encounter a wild
animal

Visits are organised by
contacting the Animal Farm
on 0114 2582452

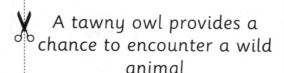 The cattle on the farm
include Highland cows,
with their long, shaggy
fringes

Chicks and ducklings can
be encountered in the
handling enclosures

One of the main costs on
the farm is the price of
animal food

Planet Paragraphs

Using the facts in the notebooks, write report paragraphs about the planet Mars and the Moon.

Mars

_____

_____

_____

_____

_____

_____

_____

Mars notebook:

Surface = dust + rocks.
Reddish, brown colour

Sometimes has large dust storms.

Ice caps at North and South pole

Named after Roman God of War

Has 2 moons

Solid, rocky surface

228 million km from sun

Volcano on Mars – called Olympus Mons – is largest volcano in solar system

The Moon

_____

_____

_____

_____

_____

_____

Moon notebook:

Has mountains, valleys and craters

Diameter 3476 km

Much less gravity – things weigh less there – $\frac{1}{6}$ of Earth's pull

81 moons weigh same as 1 earth

Largest crater = 290 km across

100°C on side facing sun

382,400 km from Earth

First person landed there: Neil Armstrong in 1969

Reflects light from sun

Circles Earth every 27 days.

Draw it – Report it

Draw something about which you are going to write a report in the middle of this page. Use the report bubbles around the edge to note down facts or features you will include in your report.

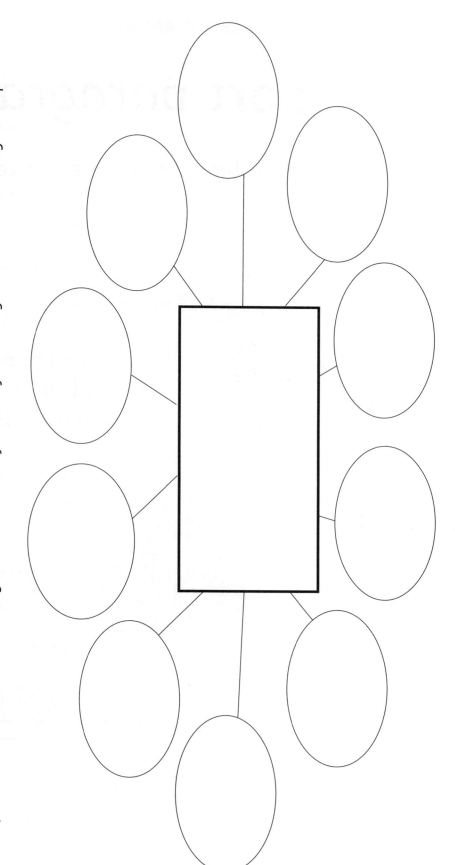

Report paragraphs

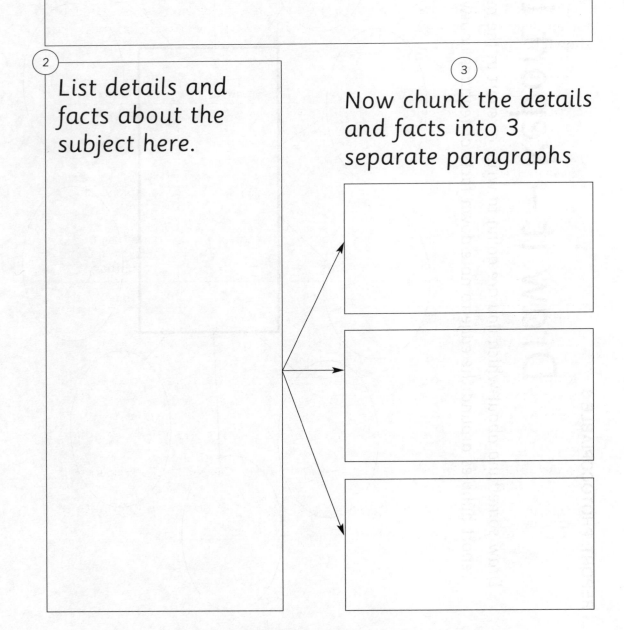

1 What is the subject of your report text?

2 List details and facts about the subject here.

3 Now chunk the details and facts into 3 separate paragraphs

5 Explanation

FEATURES OF TEXT TYPE

When we need to provide an account of how something works we use the 'explanation' genre. As the name suggests this genre *explains* or gives reasons for an event or process. Some typical features of the explanation genre are shown below.

	Text	Sentence	Word
Explanation *E.g.: a textbook explaining scientific phenomena, or an explanatory letter.*	• logical progression of statements which explain a process • begin by stating the phenomenon or by asking a question • may use diagrams	• simple present tense • temporal or causal connectives • passive sentences	• generic participants and locations • verbs describing actions and processes • technical or subject-specific vocabulary

---

Quick guide to terminology

causal connectives – connectives indicating cause and effect (e.g. 'as a result'; 'so'; 'because')

simple present tense – verbs that describe actions, events or processes that apply 'now' (e.g. 'hamsters make good pets' or 'the balloon floats on water')

passive sentences – sentences in which the subject is passive (e.g. 'the rocks are worn away by the action of water'; or 'the rocks are worn away', in which 'rocks' is the subject)

temporal connectives – connectives indicating the passage of time (e.g. 'meanwhile', 'later', 'afterwards')

generic participants – nouns that refer to a group of objects (e.g. 'plants' or 'buildings')

SHARED TEXT

Explanation: The water cycle

In the water cycle, water evaporates up from the earth then precipitates back down.

The process involves evaporation. Water in seas and lakes, or even puddles, is warmed by the sun. As a result liquid water evaporates into a gas, known as water vapour. This rises into the atmosphere where it is carried by the air. When this vapour cools it forms clouds. Precipitation happens when these clouds drop the water back onto the earth as a liquid (rain) or solid (snow and hail). This fallen water begins to flow into rivers and seas and, once again, evaporation is at work. It would take a million years for all the water in the world's oceans to pass through this cycle.

The fallen water is evaporated, condenses into clouds and precipitates again and again, making a cycle.

ANNOTATED SHARED TEXT

begin by stating the phenomenon or by asking a question	In the water cycle, water evaporates up from the earth then precipitates back down.	simple present tense
	The process involves evaporation. Water in seas and lakes, or even puddles, is warmed by the sun. As a result liquid water evaporates into a gas, known as water vapour. This rises into the atmosphere where it is carried by the air. When this vapour cools it forms clouds. Precipitation happens when these clouds drop the water back onto the earth as a liquid (rain) or solid (snow and hail). This fallen water begins to flow into rivers and seas and, once again, evaporation is at work. It would take a million years for all the water in the world's oceans to pass through this cycle.	generic participants and locations (e.g. 'rivers' rather than a specific river)
logical progression of statements which explain a process		passive sentences: 'is warmed by'
		causal connectives: 'as a result'
		temporal connectives: 'then . . . when'
	The fallen water is evaporated, condenses into clouds and precipitates again and again, making a cycle.	technical or subject-specific vocabulary
		verbs describing actions and processes

TEACHER'S NOTES

Shared Explanation Text: The Water Cycle

The water cycle is a typical example of a process. Writing about such processes, fitting the pattern of cause and effect, involves the production of an explanatory text. The two essential elements in such texts are:

- stages in such a process, e.g. forming clouds, vapour cooling
- connections between the stages, e.g. 'when this vapour cools it forms clouds'.

As they read this text children can begin to locate the various stages in the process. Imagining they were a drop of water, what various stages would they go through?

Children can use the vocabulary in the text as a way of focusing on these twin features. Ask them to locate and list the technical vocabulary in the text, including all the subject-specific words such as 'clouds' and 'cools'. Once they have produced this ask how the text links one word to another, e.g. 'vapour forms clouds'. The connection of one thing leading to another is the explanatory purpose of the text, connecting and explaining.

SAMPLE TEXTS

Sample Text A: How the projector works

The specific steps presented here connect together to explain how a projector works. This text presents another clear example of the interrelationship between various parts of a process. The bulb and shutter connect together to project the film.

Before they read the text children should recall the experience of visiting the cinema and discuss what awareness they already have of the projection process.

After they have read this they could be encouraged to write their own 'How it Works' text, explaining the workings of a gadget or machine with which they are familiar.

Sample Text B: Wild Thing!

Unlike the projector text this example presents the explanation of a daily routine.

The generic nature of such texts emerges in this example. This is a specific person writing about the programme she operates on particular days with specific otters. However, the text is explaining what generally happens rather than telling the story of a specific otter, hence the use of the generic 'otters'.

ACTIVITIES

Photocopiable 1

'Projector Quiz'. Children can cut these questions out and lay them face down on the carpet. Working in twos they take turns to pick up and read a question. They should try to answer the question using the explanation text in Photocopiable 1.

Photocopiable 2

'Connecting explanations'. Causal links in the 'Wild thing!' text provide a good example of the way in which explanation links one thing to another.

Photocopiable 3

'How the bike works'. Based on their reading of the projector example, children can use these stages to explain a technical process with which they will be more familiar, the movement of a bicycle. This should be cut out rather than numbered on the page, giving children the opportunity to rearrange the rectangles as they re-read the text.

Writing

Explanations can outline any process, a fact that opens up writing activities to more than just technical or scientific fields.

- Routines can be explained. The morning routine of collecting dinner money and filling in registers can provide material for an explanation of how and why such processes operate. Children could write for a real audience, producing explanations for a supply teacher or other staff relating the routines of classroom life.
- Children should develop their construction of cause and effect sentences as a basis for writing explanations. This involves producing sentences in which there are causal linking words, such as 'because' or 'this is so that...'. Keep a list of the causal links they find in texts they read and encourage children to draw on these in their writing. (Creating such a list can become an interesting staff development task.)
- Gadgets and simple machines, such as tin openers, corkscrews and hand drills provide interesting material to use in producing simple explanations of how things work. Bring in a pile of simple gadgets, such as hole punches, staplers and clothes pegs and ask children to think through the different

parts of the process of using these and the effect they have, then produce simple explanatory texts with supporting diagrams.

- Question and answer sessions can focus on areas of explanation with which children are already familiar. If they have worked on a process such as the water cycle, they can try producing a set of questions, something akin to the Projector Quiz (Photocopiable 1).
- Cycles and life processes lend themselves to good material for the writing of explanation. Such writing should always be preceded by a plan that shows the flow of events, with one thing leading to another, before the text is written up.

PLANNER

Photocopiable Planner

The photocopiable presents some of the causal linking words and phrases that can be used in explanation writing. These act like links in a chain. Children are asked to find causes and effects that can be placed on either side of the central link. The suggested phrases are only a start. New chains can be made out of other connecting words and phrases encountered in reading and discussion. A bank of individual chains can be stored centrally, resourcing a whole class (or key stage) project to find and use the largest number of connectives.

As they undertake this task you should clarify with the children the direction the process is taking. Is the link on the left the cause or the effect? In the example 'The wind blew so the flag waved' it is the cause. In 'The flag waved because the wind blew' it is the effect.

How the projector works

1 The reels of film are delivered in large cans.

2 The reels are joined or 'spliced' together and wound onto a platter so that the film can run through the projector in one go.

3 The film can then be 'laced up' which means threaded through rollers and run through the projector.

4 A very powerful light bulb and a mirror send the light through the shutter.

5 The shutter is a hole with a rotating blade that opens and closes the hole 24 times a second.

6 The film is passed in front of the shutter so that each frame is in place just as the shutter opens.

7 The light is then passed through a lens which focuses the image onto the screen.

8 The film is then run back on a different platter ready to use again.

© UCI Cinemas

49

Wild thing!

Grace's otter cub rehab programme!

When baby otters first arrive they are kept inside, often with a heat lamp. That's because a cub will die if it gets too cold. Otters are much better at being bottle-fed than seals. Seals suck on anything but a bottle, so you have to give them a stomach tube.

Next, the cubs are moved to a small pen with a heated shed. It has an outrun, so they can get outside and take a dip in the pool.

At six months, we move them to pens away from the hospital. They're still fenced in, but it's like living in the wild and we only feed them once a day.

When they're about a year old, we release them. This is when their mothers would let them go in the wild.

Once the otters are released, we keep monitoring them and, so far, we haven't had any problems. We have used radio tracking, but generally we just keep an eye on them – and, yes, we can tell them apart! We ask people on the island to keep an eye out for them, too.

From *The Times meg@*, July 1st, 2000

Projector Quiz

You can use these questions to test your understanding of the explanation, 'How the Projector Works'.

Why must a film be spliced?

What does the lens do?

When does each frame need to be in place?

What does 'laced up' mean?

Why is a film 'laced up'?

What are the reels of film delivered in?

Why is a light passed through the shutter?

What is the image focused and projected on?

What does 'spliced' mean?

How is the film made ready to use again?

Connecting explanations

In explanations one thing explains another. Cut out the mixed facts below. Connect the facts that explain or are explained by another.

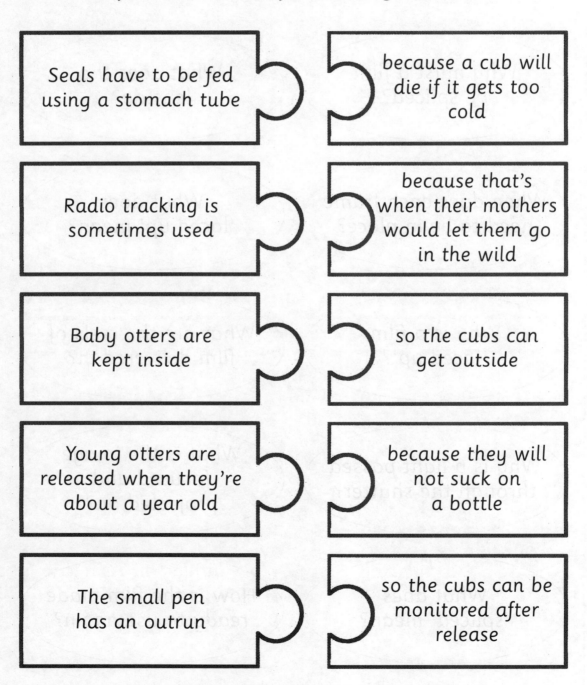

Seals have to be fed using a stomach tube	because a cub will die if it gets too cold
Radio tracking is sometimes used	because that's when their mothers would let them go in the wild
Baby otters are kept inside	so the cubs can get outside
Young otters are released when they're about a year old	because they will not suck on a bottle
The small pen has an outrun	so the cubs can be monitored after release

How the bike works

Cut out the steps explaining how a bicycle works. Sort them in to the correct order. Number the explanation steps.

○ To stop the bike moving forwards the rider squeezes a brake lever

brake lever
brake lever

○ As the chain moves it turns the back wheel, moving the bike forwards

○ Once it is moving forwards, handlebars turn the front wheel and steer the bike

○ The pedals turn a jagged edged wheel called the chain wheel
chain
wheel

○ The rider pushes down on the pedal
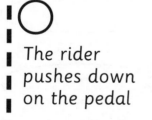

○ This lever connects to two rubber pads alongside the front wheel
brake pads

○ When the lever is squeezed the pads press against the wheel, stopping the bike

○ The chain wheel turning moves a long chain connected to the back wheel

Linking to Explain

Try making sentences with the link word in the middle. The
sentences will link together one thing caused by another.

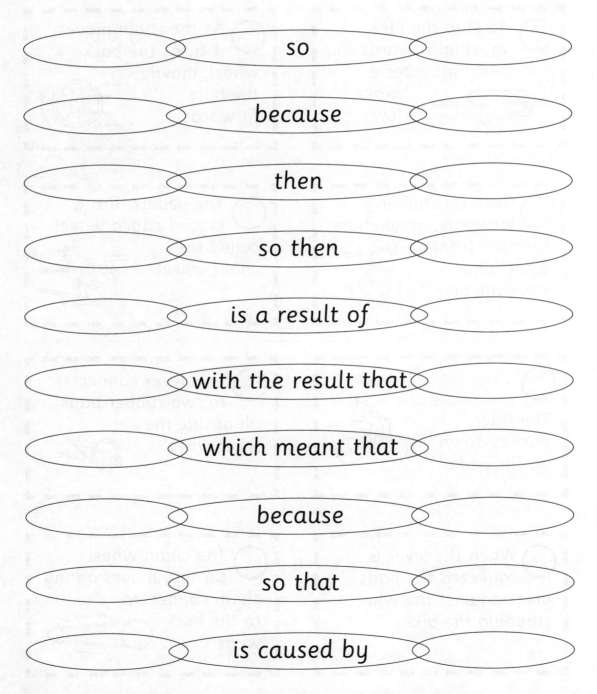

so

because

then

so then

is a result of

with the result that

which meant that

because

so that

is caused by

© Guy Merchant and Huw Thomas (2001) *Non-Fiction for the Literacy Hour*

6 Instruction

FEATURES OF TEXT TYPE

Describing a sequence of actions or a procedure is the essence of the instruction genre. Instructions help us to get things done and therefore relate well to practical activity in the classroom. Some typical features of the instruction genre are shown below.

	Text	Sentence	Word
Instruction *E.g.: recipe, manual, instructions for a game.*	• organised in chronological sequence detailing a number of stages • lists of materials or parts • states the goal, the materials and the method	• imperative sentences • adverbial clauses • temporal and causal connectives • simple sentences • lists or numbered sentences	• generic participants and locations • although the reader may be directly addressed through the use of personal pronouns • prepositions

Quick guide to terminology

adverbial clauses – clauses of time, place or manner (e.g. 'after a few days'; 'by the side of an old farmhouse')

causal connectives – connectives indicating cause and effect (e.g. 'as a result'; 'so'; 'because')

chronological sequence – texts in which there is a clear sense of the order of events

imperative sentences – sentences used to instruct or direct beginning with a verb (e.g. '*Squeeze* the glue onto the cardboard'; '*Align* the two sections', in which verbs are italicised)

personal pronouns – words used to refer to specific participants (e.g. 'I/me'; 'she/him'; 'they/them')

prepositions – words used to indicate time, position or method (e.g. 'during'; 'on'; 'under'; 'by'; 'with')

temporal connectives – connectives indicating the passage of time (e.g. 'meanwhile', 'later', 'afterwards')

SHARED TEXT

Instruction: Flick cartoon

How to make a Flick cartoon
You will need: a slip of paper
a pen or pencil

Here's how to make a simple picture that moves, just like a cartoon film.

What to do
First fold the strip of paper in half.

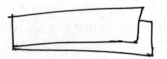

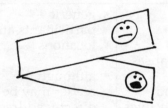

On the open end of the strip draw a picture, then open the strip and draw a similar picture with a slight change.

Hint: It could be a face with eyes open in one picture and closed in another.

Roll the top slip around the pen, very tightly. Hold it like this for 15 seconds.

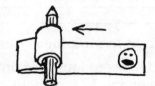

Release the pen.
After this, the top strip should now be like a spring.

Slide the pen along the top strip so it unwinds and winds quickly. The pictures should flick from one to another, as if the picture is moving.

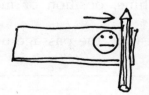
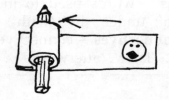

ANNOTATED SHARED TEXT

lists of materials or parts states the goal	### How to make a Flick cartoon *You will need: a slip of paper* *a pen or pencil* *Here's how to make a simple picture that moves, just like a cartoon film.*	generic participants and locations e.g. 'you will need' – the reader is being directly addressed through the use of personal pronouns

What to do
First fold the strip of paper in half.

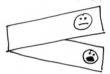

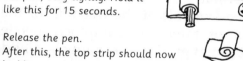

On the open end of the strip draw a picture, then open the strip and draw a similar picture with a slight change.

> *Hint: It could be a face with eyes open in one picture and closed in another.*

Roll the top slip around the pen, very tightly. Hold it like this for 15 seconds.

Release the pen.
After this, the top strip should now be like a spring.

Slide the pen along the top strip so it unwinds and winds quickly. The pictures should flick from one to another, as if the picture is moving.

(left column, lower)
organised in chronological sequence detailing a number of stages

(right column, lower)
imperative sentences, e.g. 'First fold...in half'

lists or numbered sentences

adverbial clauses, e.g. 'very tightly' . . .

temporal connectives, e.g. 'After this . . .'

prepositions, e.g. 'along, from . . . to'

causal connectives, e.g. 'so . . .'

TEACHER'S NOTES

Shared Instruction Text: Flick cartoon

The text on making a flick cartoon should not be read. It should be followed. The real reading of such a text lies in following the instructions it issues.

One way of doing this is to issue the text to the class as a shared text, with the necessary materials and ask them to work in pairs achieving the eventual aim.

As they do this some will stumble and struggle, others will progress. You could add the possibility that they can help each other on the condition that they use the words from the text. Anyone showing someone else how to do a part of the task has to refer to the text for the instruction that lies behind their action.

Point out the way in which the structure and connectives in the text guide the reader through a step by step process.

SAMPLE TEXTS

Sample Text A: Endings game

Once again, a text to be followed if it is to be really read.

One way in which they can develop their reading of this text is for children to try fitting games they already know or play at school, such as 'Kim's Game', into the same instruction format.

Ask them to interpret the symbols at the opening of the text (number of players, mode of play, type of game and equipment needed). A lot of non-narrative texts, such as restaurant guides, use symbols. Children could discuss why this might be the case.

This text provides a useful example of the use of generic participants (e.g. 'Players can take…') rather than direct pronouns (e.g. 'You can take…').

Sample Text B: Historic Eyam

The Historic Eyam walk provides an alternative use of instructional texts to direct a participant through a specific route. Two interesting features that merit some interpretation are the use of a number of symbols and conventions and the constant use of imperative verbs, without generic participants. This is because the text is meant to be read as part of the task and to point the reader in a more direct way along their path.

ACTIVITIES

Photocopiable 1

'Endings Game'. This photocopiable develops the challenge of the endings game. It supports the reading of the text by presenting a set of word endings, enabling children to supply three words for each.

Photocopiable 2

'Follow the Symbols'. Returning to the symbols in the Historic Eyam walk, this photocopiable asks children to figure out what they think the symbols might mean. Once they have written in their guesses they can compare notes and see if they came up with similar guesses. The answers are given on p. 97.

Photocopiable 3

'Letter list' and 'Guess Me'. The two sets of games instructions on this photocopiable provide further reading of the games instructions as presented in Sample Text A. These should be attempted independently, beginning with the text and trying to figure out the game, then sharing the playing with others who have followed the same process. The effective reading of an instructional text should be evident in the common result.

Writing

The production of procedural texts is rooted in having a good task with which the children are familiar. This is vital if the planning is to be effective. The science or technology task they have just undertaken is not half as good in terms of subject matter for this writing as the game or activity with which they are familiar, such as making a sandwich or filling in the register. One of the main points to emphasise in constructing this type of writing is the need for a clear use of step by step processes to structure the final text. Activities can include:

- A route walk along the lines of the Historic Eyam text. This could involve a route between home and school or from home to the local shop. If children do this in guided writing groups they can undertake the added challenge of coming up with a set of symbols that will work for the environment in which their walks are to be set.
- Games boxes can provide an interesting source for this activity. In many classrooms there are well known games, such as Connect 4, for which the instructions are long since lost. Ask children to replace the missing instructions.

- Instructional writing is open to some entertaining parodies which all serve to reinforce the structure of the text. Ask children to produce texts along the lines of 'How to Trap a Giant' or 'How to Get Out of Trouble'.
- Tricks and practical jokes are a good source of subject matter for this sort of writing. Children can collect examples from adults at home and other members of staff and try writing up their own book of tricks.

PLANNER

Photocopiable Planner

The planner looks at the basic task and how it is to be structured. The notes on what you have to do must be made before writing in the step by step process.

INSTRUCTION: SAMPLE TEXT A

Endings Game

Endings

 Two or more players

 Challenge game

✍ Played by writing or speaking

✎ Played with pencils and paper, or with no equipment

Object To think of words with particular endings.

Procedure This game can be played in two ways. Players can take turns to ask other players to think of a word that ends with a particular series of letters. Alternatively, players can be given a list of word endings and challenged to write down one word for each ending. The winner is the first player to write down suitable words for the whole list.

Example

TONY: Can you think of a word that ends with –RY?

KATE: *Try.*

ANNA: *Inquiry.*

CHAS: *Descry.* Can you think of a word that ends with –YER?

TONY: *Player.*

KATE: *Soothsayer.*

ANNA: *Lawyer.* Can you give me a word that ends with –CEFUL?

CHAS: *Resourceful.*

TONY: *Peaceful.*

KATE: *Disgraceful.* Can you think of a word that ends with –UIA?

ANNA: *Alleluia.*

CHAS: *Colloquia.*

TONY: I can't think of one. (*He has to drop out of the game.*)

Also called Word Endings.

From *The Oxford A–Z of Word Games* by Tony Augarde. Published by Oxford University Press (1995)

Historic Eyam

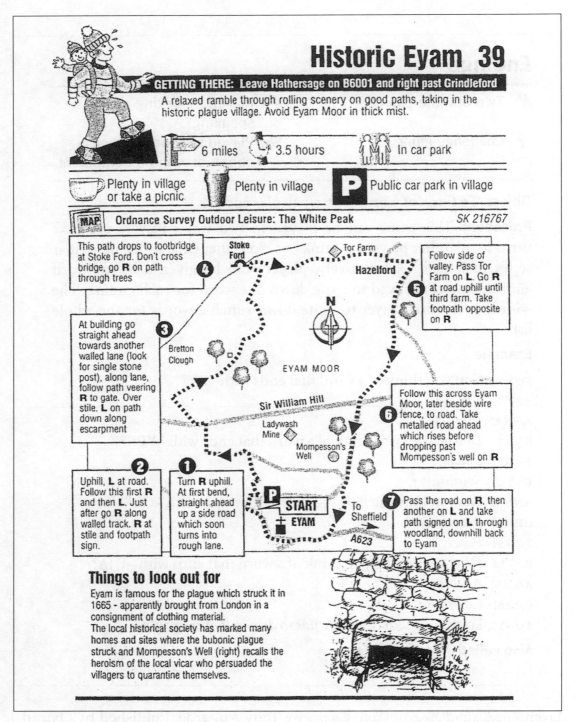

Historic Eyam 39

GETTING THERE: Leave Hathersage on B6001 and right past Grindleford

A relaxed ramble through rolling scenery on good paths, taking in the historic plague village. Avoid Eyam Moor in thick mist.

6 miles | 3.5 hours | In car park

Plenty in village or take a picnic | Plenty in village | **P** Public car park in village

MAP Ordnance Survey Outdoor Leisure: The White Peak | SK 216767

4 This path drops to footbridge at Stoke Ford. Don't cross bridge, go **R** on path through trees

3 At building go straight ahead towards another walled lane (look for single stone post), along lane, follow path veering **R** to gate. Over stile. **L** on path down along escarpment

5 Follow side of valley. Pass Tor Farm on **L**. Go **R** at road uphill until third farm. Take footpath opposite on **R**

6 Follow this across Eyam Moor, later beside wire fence, to road. Take metalled road ahead which rises before dropping past Mompesson's well on **R**

2 Uphill, **L** at road. Follow this first **R** and then **L**. Just after go **R** along walled track. **R** at stile and footpath sign.

1 Turn **R** uphill. At first bend, straight ahead up a side road which soon turns into rough lane.

7 Pass the road on **R**, then another on **L** and take path signed on **L** through woodland, downhill back to Eyam

Stoke Ford
Tor Farm
Hazelford
Bretton Clough
EYAM MOOR
N
Sir William Hill
Ladywash Mine
Mompesson's Well
P START + EYAM
To Sheffield
A623

Things to look out for

Eyam is famous for the plague which struck it in 1665 - apparently brought from London in a consignment of clothing material.

The local historical society has marked many homes and sites where the bubonic plague struck and Mompesson's Well (right) recalls the heroism of the local vicar who persuaded the villagers to quarantine themselves.

from *The Star Family Walks* by John Spencer and Ann Beedham

Endings Game

Here are some 'Endings' as in the game
'Endings' in the instructions on p. 54.
Try thinking of three words for each ending.

	word 1	word 2	word 3
ing			
er			
ed			
ful			
ged			
able			
ost			
ance			
ale			
ight			
ibble			
ves			

Follow the Symbols

Pick out these symbols on the map of Historic Eyam. What do you think they stand for?

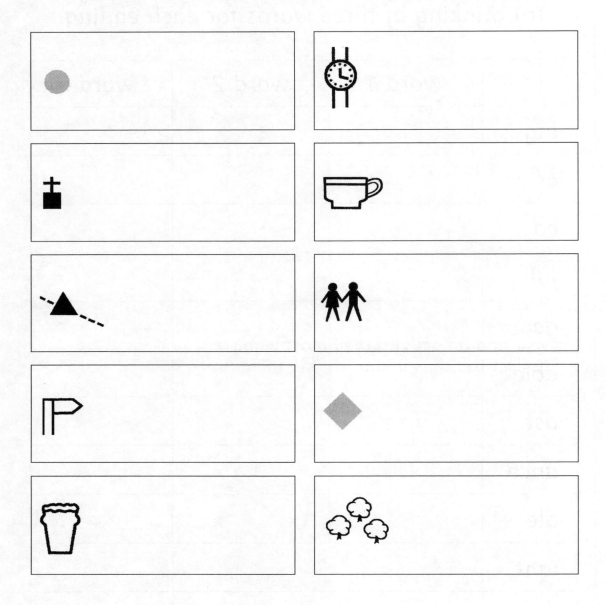

Letter list

for 4 to 7 players

You will need:
Pencils, paper, a timer or second hand on a clock.

1. Each player selects a letter from the alphabet and writes it on a scrap of paper, without letting the other players see it.
2. When everyone is ready, someone says 'Go'. Each player then shows their letter.
3. The players then have one minute in which to make a sentence that uses each of the letters shown – and no more.

Guess Me

for 4 to 6 players

You will need:
Pencils, 3 slips of paper for each player.

- Each player has to write on their slips of paper the following: their favourite food, a place they would like to visit and an activity they most enjoy.
- Collect the slips in and shuffle them up.
- Deal out the slips, without looking at what is written on them. Each player should now have three slips.
- Take turns to select a slip. As each player selects one of their slips they have to say what is written on it and 'Guess me...' followed by the name of the player they thought wrote it.

> For example: If a player reads 'chips' on a slip and guesses Jo wrote it, she would say 'Chips – Guess me Jo'.

- If the Guess is right the slip can be put back in the centre. If the slip is wrong the player keeps the slip and guessing passes to the next player.
- The first player to get rid of all their slips wins.

Procedural Planner

What are you
going to do?

Opening sentence

Can you turn this into a
clear opening sentence? →

Notes on what you
will need:

Can you organise these
into a good list? →

Notes on what you
have to do:

Can you organise these
into a few clear steps?

1 _____
_____

2 _____
_____

3 _____
_____

4 _____
_____

5 _____
_____

6 _____
→ _____

7 Discussion

FEATURES OF TEXT TYPE

Discussion texts are quite closely associated with educational contexts. The most common form of discussion is the essay, in which different aspects of a debate are explored, compared and contrasted. A point of view is put forward, supported by argument or evidence. Some typical features of the discussion genre are shown below.

	Text	Sentence	Word
Discussion *E.g.: essays and some newspaper articles.*	• statement of contentious issue • two sides of the debate are presented with supporting evidence • ends with questions or conclusions • use of subheadings	• topic sentences to orientate the reader • a variety of cohesive devices including logical, additional and oppositional connectives • passive sentences	• simple present tense • generic participants (human or non-human), abstract issues, ideas or opinions • subject-specific terminology • comparative adjectives • modal verbs

Quick guide to terminology

additional connectives – connectives that indicate additional information (e.g. 'also'; 'furthermore')
comparative adjectives – adjectives that express comparison (e.g. 'better'; 'safer'; 'healthier')
logical connectives – connectives used to develop an argument (e.g. 'the reason for this'; 'therefore'; 'because of')
modal verbs – verbs that express possibility, likelihood, etc. (e.g. 'can'; 'will'; 'shall'; 'may'; 'must')
oppositional connectives – connectives that indicate contrast (e.g. 'however'; 'nevertheless'; 'on the other hand')
passive sentences – sentences in which the subject is passive (e.g. 'the rocks are worn away by the action of water'; or 'the rocks are worn away', in which 'rocks' is the subject)
topic sentences – sentences which act as signposts to the reader, introducing a particular topic (usually found at the beginning of paragraphs)

SHARED TEXT

Discussion: Teaching?

Being a teacher is a challenging job. The question is whether it's too challenging. Is teaching worth it? On the one hand there are teachers who can list their complaints. They are poorly paid and made to work long hours. Some teachers feel children don't respect them. A number of teachers feel there is too much paperwork involved in their job.

On the other hand there are teachers who say it is a rewarding job and enjoy seeing children learn. They like working in schools where they often get on well with their colleagues. In addition, some would say that teachers get good holidays. It is a fact that teachers get more holiday than most other professions, particularly during the summer.

It could be that there is a balance here. For some teachers the amount of work they do is balanced by the satisfaction they get from the job. Others find the good holidays balanced by having to prepare lesson plans and timetables for the coming term.

It would seem there is a balancing act taking place, between the good and bad things to be found in this job.

ANNOTATED SHARED TEXT

		simple present tense – note use of 'is', 'are', 'can'
		generic participants, e.g. 'teachers', 'children'
statement of contentious issue	Being a teacher is a challenging job. The question is whether it's too challenging. Is teaching worth it? On the one hand there are teachers who can list their complaints. They are poorly paid and made to work long hours. Some teachers feel children don't respect them. A number of teachers feel there is too much paperwork involved in their job.	abstract issues, e.g. 'teaching'
		passive sentences, 'They are poorly paid'
two sides of the debate are presented with supporting evidence	On the other hand there are teachers who say it is a rewarding job and enjoy seeing children learn. They like working in schools where they often get on well with their colleagues. In addition, some would say that teachers get good holidays. It is a fact that teachers get more holiday than most other professions, particularly during the summer.	topic sentences to orientate the reader
	It could be that there is a balance here. For some teachers the amount of work they do is balanced by the satisfaction they get from the job. Others find the good holidays balanced by having to prepare lesson plans and timetables for the coming term.	modal verbs, e.g. 'some *would* say', '*could* be that'
ends with questions or conclusions	It would seem there is a balancing act taking place, between the good and bad things to be found in this job.	a variety of cohesive devices, e.g. *'on the other hand'*, *'in addition'*
		subject-specific terminology, e.g. 'lesson plans', 'timetables'
		comparative adjectives

TEACHER'S NOTES

Shared Discussion Text: Teaching?

This text raises the issue of teaching as a career, presenting two sides of the case.

Children can locate within this text a structuring of two sides, with a basic for and against followed by a balancing of the argument.

The best way to begin reading a text like this is to avoid analysing the framing of the two sides of the argument. Instead, children should enter into the debate. Having read the text how would they respond? What points would they make about this issue that are missing from this text?

One important aspect of this text is the way it can keep an issue in abstract and provisional terms. These sorts of texts are explorations rather than clear statements. They include facts, such as the statement about teacher holidays, but balance these with the fact that the issue under discussion is still not decided, hence the use of modal verbs such as 'could' and 'would' and the use of abstract language.

Children could create a simple list of points on the two sides of the issue, for and against teaching, and add points of their own. They could also explore the responses of other teachers to this text, collecting any responses or points made by staff in school following a reading of the text.

SAMPLE TEXTS

Sample Text A: Talking points

The format of this text is interesting, giving clear For and Against sections. The points are kept separate and set against each other in a stark opposition. Children might want to take this text as a starting point and, in a shared writing exercise, suggest various sentences that could be used to end the text. Look back at the closing sentence in 'Teaching?', drawing the strands of the argument together. Can they provide a similar, balanced closure for the argument?

Sample Text B: Gangs

In this text the two sides of the argument are merged within the same paragraphs, providing a contrast to the Talking Points article. Children could try structuring the 'For' and 'Against' points for Gangs in a similar way to the Talking Points text.

ACTIVITIES

Photocopiable 1

'Sort the argument'. This activity asks children to work with both the Sample Texts A and B, finding the points that are made to counter those shown in the arrows. To do this children will need to work out which issue the points made in the first arrow concern. They then need to find a point made in the text that argues against the arrow. Having done this they can cut out arrow shapes of their own and create similar oppositions between points in an argument. These could be further ones drawn from the texts. They could also use the shared text, 'Teaching?', as their starting point.

Photocopiable 2

'Answer to discuss'. This activity isn't just about comprehending Sample Text B. It involves children thinking through their own responses, following their reflection on the text.

Photocopiable 3

'Opinions'. These discussion starters provide a statement and a question for discussion. The point to stress here is that there is a skill to not closing the issue in the first sentence. Faced with the question whether strict teachers are better, children should aim to move beyond a simple 'Yes' or 'No' to seeing that points can be made for and against the statement. A good discussion text aims to tease out these two sides.

Writing

Discussion texts are difficult to compose. Children struggle with putting themselves in the shoes of the other side in the argument, figuring how they might react to an issue and expressing an alternative side to an argument. Writing can be enhanced in a number of ways:

- It is vital to remember that discussion texts involve discussion. Planning such a text should not be a solitary activity. Children should contribute and discuss their views around an issue.
- Finding the right subject matter is an essential part of this activity. Current issues, such as local or national debates, can provide a good starting point. Children can be furnished with opposing pieces from divergent tabloids as

a basis for such exploration. It is always useful to find staff who are prepared to wade in on either side of an issue. Possibilities include

Should smoking in public be banned?

Is meat eating wrong?

If cars pollute should petrol be very expensive?

Are there too many quiz shows on television?

- Role playing sides is a vital starting point. Rather than asking children to express their own opinion, they need to express what another person with a different view might say. If they are staunchly vegetarian, they need to enter the composition of an argument on the morality of killing animals for food, by thinking what a meat eater, beef farmer or butcher might say. One way of doing this is to ask children to role play such stances in a class discussion.

- 'I think' starters can provide the makings of discussion material. These involve staff or children writing an opinion (e.g. 'School dinners are no good') in the middle of a large piece of paper. These papers are left out in the classroom, or passed around groups at work, with the aim that others should add their views or questions around the central point (e.g. 'All dinners or particular ones?', 'Some people like them'). The writer who started the argument can return and respond to selected points. If these are passed between classes or staff they can add some good extended material.

- Websites devoted to responding to the news can provide some good, up-to-date discussion on current issues. These can provide the basis for constructing the views around an issue.

PLANNER

Photocopiable Planner

This planner presents space to express an issue, collate points around it and provide summative thoughts. It avoids the words 'For' and 'Against', as the two sides to an issue are not always as simple as these terms would imply.

Talking points

Winning a gold metal is important, but is winning everything?

For

What is the point of sport if you don't try hard to win? <u>There have to be losers</u>, <u>so there can be winners</u>. Playing to win is a noble aim. Stakes are high because successful sports stars can become millionaires. Spectators love the drama of winning and losing. Who would watch 'collaborative' football?

Against

Taking part is as important as winning. Many people just want to be fit. Too much adulation for winners demeans the millions who never win. People drop out of sport in their thirties, when <u>they could play for decades</u> if winning were less important. Stress on medals leads to <u>cheating</u>. Nationalism is unhealthy.

Gangs

© Aladdin Books Ltd 1996. Julie Johnson, *How Do I Feel about Bullies and Gangs?*

Sort the argument

Look in the two discussion texts to find parts that argue against these views.

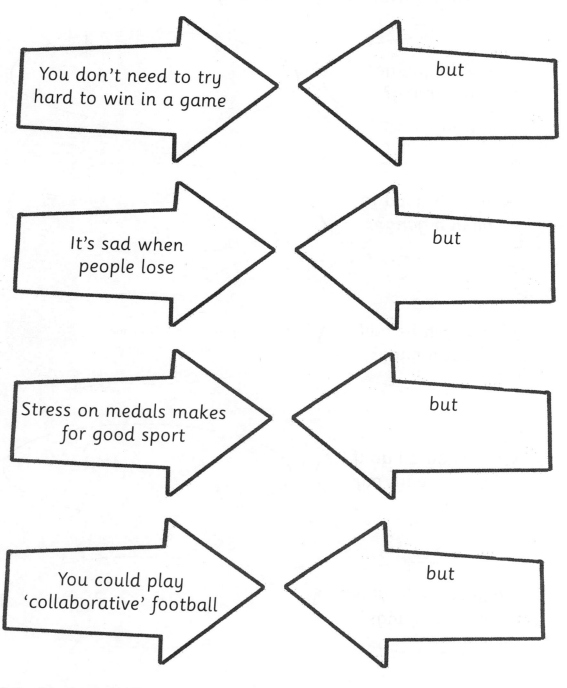

You don't need to try hard to win in a game

but

It's sad when people lose

but

Stress on medals makes for good sport

but

You could play 'collaborative' football

but

Answer to discuss

Discussion is about answering one opinion with another. Read 'Gangs' then look at these questions. How would you respond?

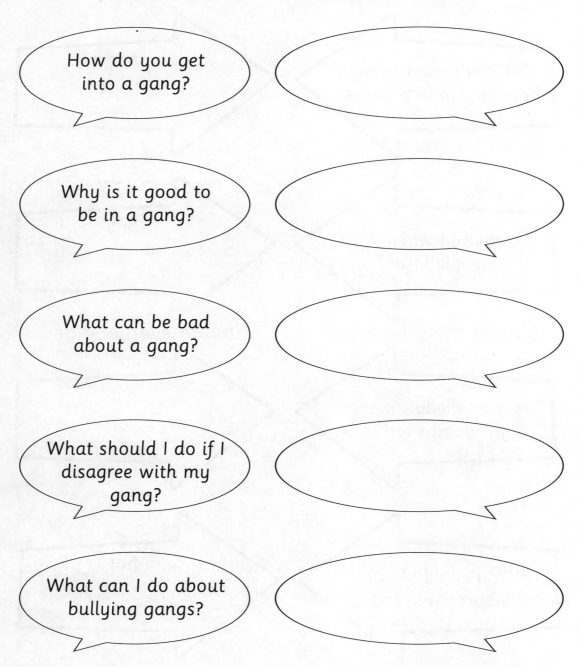

How do you get into a gang?

Why is it good to be in a gang?

What can be bad about a gang?

What should I do if I disagree with my gang?

What can I do about bullying gangs?

Opinions

Children need to do a certain number of hours at school.

Would we be better having shorter breaks and lunch times and going home earlier?

Teachers need to keep discipline and should make learning enjoyable.

Are strict teachers better?

Lots of people like football, but a lot don't.

Should there be more football on television?

Doctors are paid more than people who drive ambulances.

Should everyone be paid differently for different jobs?

Petrol fumes are bad for the environment.

Should the Government stop people using their cars as much as they do?

Parents want to help their children plan for the future.

Should your parents have a say in the job you choose?

© Guy Merchant and Huw Thomas (2001) *Non-Fiction for the Literacy Hour*

Discussion planner

Issue

Side A   Side B

Thoughts on the issue

8 Persuasion

FEATURES OF TEXT TYPE

This category actually covers quite a broad range of text types that aim to influence the way you think or act. Advertisements usually attempt to persuade you to buy a particular product by making it sound attractive, whereas other persuasive texts may simply aim to influence the way you think or live your life. Some typical features of the discussion genre are shown in the table.

	Text	Sentence	Word
Persuasion *E.g.: public information posters, advertising leaflets, magazine articles.*	• slogan or short sentence that highlights the topic or product • opening statement followed by a justification of point of view/issue/ product • problem–solution pattern • careful use of visual images and layout	• simple, catchy sentences (or wordplay) • statements of fact or opinion • imperative sentences • causal connectives	• simple present tense • generic classes of objects (e.g. wildlife) or specific proper nouns (e.g. brand names) • interaction with the use of personal pronouns ('we' and 'you') • modal verbs

Quick guide to terminology

causal connectives – connectives indicating cause and effect (e.g. 'as a result'; 'so'; 'because')

imperative sentences – sentences used to instruct or direct, beginning with a verb (e.g. '*Squeeze* the glue onto the cardboard'; '*Align* the two sections', in which verbs are italicised)

modal verbs – verbs that express possibility, likelihood, etc. (e.g. 'can'; 'will'; 'shall'; 'may'; 'must')

personal pronouns – words used to refer to specific participants (e.g. 'I/me'; 'she/him'; 'they/them')

SHARED TEXT

Persuasion: Toy advert, Bad advert

Toy ads are bad ads.

Television toy adverts should be banned. Television adverts for toys are unhelpful and misleading. They also cause problems between parents and children. There are a number of reasons why they should be banned.

Firstly, the adverts make children want whatever toy they are shown, whether or not their family can afford it. Children are shown other children enjoying a toy and made to feel as if they want it. The music and songs bombard children's senses so that they can think of nothing other than the toys they are seeing. In Britain, the average child is bombarded with 18,000 such adverts a year.

Some would say adverts just provide information for children. However, adverts always make the toys look a lot better than they really are. Action figures are shown in exciting landscapes, magical figures are shown against glittering backgrounds. We all know these adverts make the toys look better than they do in real life.

Studies have shown they find it hard to tell adverts apart from actual programmes. They can end up trusting the adverts and believing they are showing the toy as it would look in real life.

Some countries have already banned toy advertising during children's programmes. It's about time everyone stopped this brainwashing of young children.

Ban these adverts now!

ANNOTATED SHARED TEXT

slogan or short sentence that highlights the topic	Toy ads are bad ads.	simple, catchy sentences
	Television toy adverts should be banned. Television adverts for toys are unhelpful and misleading. They also cause problems between parents and children. There are a number of reasons why they should be banned.	modal verbs, e.g. 'should' simple present tense: *'cause'*, *'make'*
opening statement followed by a justification of point of view/issue/ product	Firstly, the adverts make children want whatever toy they are shown, whether or not their family can afford it. Children are shown other children enjoying a toy and made to feel as if they want it. The music and songs bombard children's senses so that they can think of nothing other than the toys they are seeing. In Britain, the average child is bombarded with 18,000 such adverts a year.	statements of fact or opinion generic classes of objects (e.g. 'children') or specific proper nouns (e.g. 'Britain')
problem–solution pattern, e.g. 'Some would say... However...'	Some would say adverts just provide information for children. However, adverts always make the toys look a lot better than they really are. Action figures are shown in exciting landscapes, magical figures are shown against glittering backgrounds. We all know these adverts make the toys look better than they do in real life.	causal connectives, e.g. 'so that' interaction with the use of personal pronouns, e.g. 'We all know...'
	Studies have shown they find it hard to tell adverts apart from actual programmes. They can end up trusting the adverts and believing they are showing the toy as it would look in real life.	
	Some countries have already banned toy advertising during children's programmes. It's about time everyone stopped this brainwashing of young children.	imperative sentences
	Ban these adverts now!	

81

TEACHER'S NOTES

Shared Text: Toy advert, Bad advert

Texts that aim to persuade are hammering home their point. Following a first read of this text ask children what emotions they think the writer might feel around this issue, asking them to justify their opinions with words and phrases drawn from the text. Note, for example, the use of words like 'bombarded' to describe children watching an advert.

Ask children if they can isolate the separate points that are being made in opposition to toy advertising. Point out, in particular, the way in which the text sets up the barest opposition to its point of view, only to knock it down again. This is a vital part of persuasive writing, anticipating objections and tackling them in advance.

SAMPLE TEXTS

Sample Text A: Galacteenies

The text provides a typical example of a persuasive text aimed at selling a product to the audience. Children can begin by listing the good points the text makes about the product. What reasons does it give for purchasing the product?

Point out the appealing language being used ('out of this world', fantastic')

Sample Text B: This is your Census!

Less advert like, but still out to persuade, this leaflet went out to homes in the UK, as part of the 2001 National Census. It provided persuasive reasons for completing the census, showing how important completion was.

This text is a good example of a range of points being made to support the basic persuasive message 'fill in the census'.

It provides an interesting contrast with the Galacteenies advert, providing a less glitzy piece of persuasion for a different audience and purpose.

ACTIVITIES

Photocopiable 1

'Advert Language'. Beginning with the 'Galacteenies' advert children can locate certain features in a range of adverts cut from magazines and newspapers.

The product name should be clear. It's worth looking at the appeal the name can hold. They are thought out in lengthy meetings with a view towards selling the product. How might they do this?

- Slogan: Catchy phrases like 'They're out of this world' fix the product in the mind of the reader.
- Instruction: The advert will sometimes tell the reader to do something, e.g. 'Collect them all'.
- Question: Another way of appealing directly is to ask the reader something, 'Do you like cream cakes?'
- Description: Words used to describe a product can be interesting to note down. Adverts will sometimes contain a well chosen adjective.
- Promise: Adverts will sometimes make a direct promise (e.g. 'An experience you will never forget') as part of their sales pitch.

Photocopiable 2

'Persuading'. Taking the standpoint of someone reluctant to fill in a census form, this text asks children to look back to the point made in the shared text, namely the way in which persuasive texts need to anticipate opposition. In this activity children can find the ways in which the census leaflet presents a case that opposes certain attitudes and opinions, persuading to the contrary.

Photocopiable 3

'Glitz words'. These advertising bubbles provide spaces for children to create short persuasive pieces, starting with a product name or campaign slogan in the rectangles and using the rest of the bubble to push their point of view. They could devise a range of chocolate bars or comics. Make sure they use the advert features listed above!

Writing

Writing a persuasive piece involves using the text features presented in the annotation. Vital to this is the elaboration of more than one reason for the point of view being put. A text like 'Galacteenies' shows how a short piece of persuasion still includes an array of points supporting the simple persuasion inherent in the text. In writing such texts:

- Children should develop a good grasp of the point or product being hammered home in the persuasion. It is sometimes said that the best advert is a good product and, to persuade for something, a writer needs to know the subject matter well.
- Anticipating contrary views is a vital part of such persuasion. Listen to adverts on the television and you will note that a number of them do this. The insurance company that promise they won't give you difficult forms or the car company that promise all sorts of things if the product breaks down in the first year. When writing a persuasive text, children should have the opposing view in mind, refer to it and explain the argument against it.
- Emotive language can be seen throughout. In the census advert there is a careful appeal to duty, but the words are still well chosen.
- Paragraphing can provide an important structuring tool in persuasive writing, just as persuasion can be a good text in which to develop paragraphing. The idea of dedicating a separate paragraph to particular points and having one in which objections to the case being made are dispensed with, can provide a way of outlining a longer persuasive text.

PLANNER

Photocopiable Planner

Beginning with an issue, this task involves children thinking through persuasive arguments and countering objections. An essential part of this is the section in which children anticipate objections and react to them.

count me in
Census2001

This is your Census!

Put yourself in the picture

The Census is a count of the whole UK population that only takes place every 10 years. Census information will be used to share out billions of pounds of public money in years to come. To make sure everyone benefits, we need the whole picture.

We all need the Census

Census information is used to benefit us all – we all need to be included so we can get the services we need in the future.

Your information is confidential

Census forms are held in the strictest confidence – and are not released for 100 years!

We all need to be included

The Census is the only complete picture of the nation we have – it is impossible to plan services for invisible people.

The only way to see the full picture

The Census is a unique set of facts and figures because it counts everyone in the country at the same time – there is no other way of capturing a complete picture of the nation.

Post it back

Simply fill in the Census form on 29 April and post it back in the reply-paid envelope.

The law says you have to fill in the Census form. If you were to refuse to complete your form properly you may be liable to prosecution.

Remember
Sunday
29
April

is Census Day

national
STATISTICS

Advert Language

Look at some types of language you find in adverts.
Can you find examples in adverts you have collected?

Product name				
Slogan				
Instruction				
Question				
Description				
Promise				

Persuading

Listen to what some people might have said about completing a census. How would this leaflet persuade them?

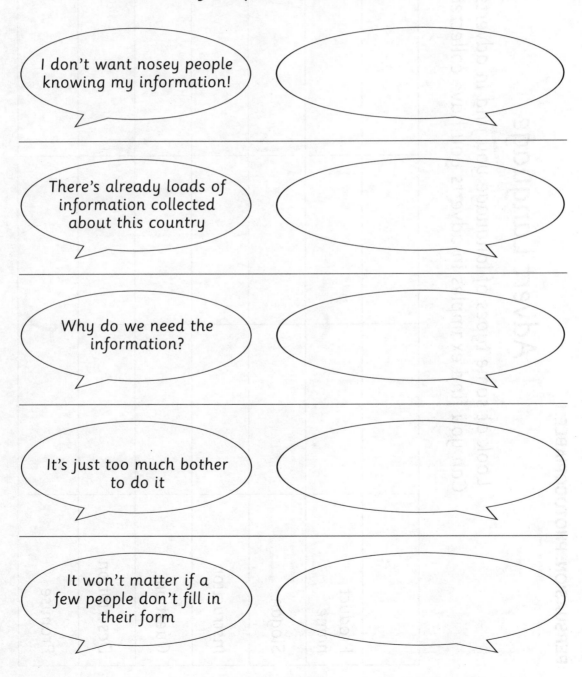

Glitz words

Plan to Persuade

What do you want to persuade a reader to think?

What are the main arguments for your persuasion?

-

-

-

How might some argue against this?	What would you say in response?

How will you finish your persuasion?

9 Developing work on non-fiction

In this chapter we draw together some important themes relating to non-fiction work in the classroom, by emphasising a systematic interpretation of the National Literacy Strategy and indicating ways of building on this. We begin by exploring three factors that promote successful classroom work: the use of texts that interest children and are relevant to their everyday life; the integration of work on text types in different curriculum areas; and an approach that encourages children to talk and think about texts, to read and act upon them, and to experiment with writing them. The chapter concludes with suggestions for extending work on non-fiction with a particular emphasis on media sources.

Understanding how texts work

In classroom work on non-fiction our fundamental aim is to help children to understand what texts mean and how that meaning is constructed. We do this to help them to learn from text and to show them how to be critical and analytical in the texts that they read and create. These aims cannot simply be achieved by working through each of the different genres but requires a sustained and systematic approach that fosters children's interest in texts themselves and engages them in discussion and activity.

The National Literacy Strategy provides a framework which encourages us to re-visit non-fiction text types on a regular basis: so, for example, you will find non-chronological reports referred to throughout Key Stages 1 and 2 (from Year 1 Term 2 to Year 6 Term 3). The challenge is to make those encounters with non-fiction motivating and meaningful for the pupils. We believe that there are three key factors in meeting this challenge. They are:

- the use of texts that interest children and that are relevant to their everyday life both in and outside the classroom;
- the integration and application of work on text types in different areas of the curriculum;
- a planning approach that allows for opportunities to talk and think about texts, to read and act upon them, and to experiment with writing them.

The following sections expand on each of these three factors in turn.

Choosing texts that are interesting and relevant

Throughout this book we have tried to place an emphasis on the use of texts that build on children's everyday experience and interest. Reliance on published scheme material, while making life easy for the busy teacher, can be a disadvantage in developing motivating non-fiction work. Although a scheme may faithfully follow termly objectives from the National Literacy Strategy framework it may not always contain material that appeals to the children you teach.

Finding out what motivates children and what holds their attention and interest is the key to successful non-fiction work. The persuasive texts that engage children are more likely to be those that relate to popular culture – the toys, games or music that are current – than the adult's conception of a good example of the genre. In a similar way, instruction texts (like the *Flick Cartoon*, in Chapter 6) that can be used to direct meaningful activity, not only demonstrate the relationship between text and action but also culminate in the production of something interesting or useful.

Applying knowledge of genre across the curriculum

As we observed in the two introductory chapters, the six text types that feature in the National Literacy Strategy framework are essentially school-based genres. The classification is based on the kinds of texts that children will need to read and write to successfully access the curriculum. In our explanation of the text types we have frequently used material from different curriculum areas. For example, we have drawn attention to the ways in which *recount* may be used in history; *explanation* in geography and *instruction* in technology.

In developing and consolidating work on the non-fiction genres, cross-curricular planning is crucial. Good teaching is about helping children to make links in their learning. Using texts from different curriculum areas as a vehicle for literacy teaching is important. This will help children to gain a deeper understanding of the subject matter as well as providing a way into looking at the language features of the particular genre. In this way, the Mary Seacole text in Chapter 3 provides a natural link with the history curriculum, whereas the Gangs text in Chapter 7 links to PSHE. Initial shared work on these texts will be about discussing the meaning, helping children to map the content on to their existing knowledge and experience. This can then be followed by specific text, sentence and word level work to develop an understanding of the text type. More detailed subject-specific work will occur elsewhere in the curriculum.

The balance between learning *from* text and learning *about* text challenges many teachers, particularly when advice or rumour has implied that subject content should not be discussed in a literacy hour (Dadds 1999). It is clearly very important that meaning making should take precedence – subject content should be discussed – but at the same time teaching and learning needs to be guided by literacy objectives or else it will be in danger of loosing its focus. Conversely, in other areas of the curriculum, children will need to be reminded of the work they have done on text types and may well use the same shared text to develop subject knowledge. For example, the instruction text Historic Eyam in Chapter 6 could be used as a starting point for map work in geography. Here the geography objective would have primacy, but links would be drawn to learning in literacy.

An integrated approach to genre-based work

Good literacy teaching is informed by an understanding of the relationship between speaking and listening, reading and writing. In non-fiction work this means that children will have opportunities to talk and think about texts, to read and act upon them, and to experiment with writing them. Building such opportunities into literacy work in a coherent way is an important aspect of planning – planning that will give children plenty of experience of *talking about text*, structured *reading of text*, follow-up *activities on text*, and support in experimenting with *creating text*. These experiences are not to be seen as a fixed teaching sequence, but simply suggest possibilities. We have found that careful thinking about these four elements can enrich teachers' planning. The planning model is based on work by Merchant and Wilkinson (Leeds LEA 1998). Figure 9.1 shows the features of each of these elements.

Talking about text	Whole-class, small group or paired discussion that supports children in jointly constructing the meaning of a text, followed by work that identifies the characteristics and linguistic features of the text.
Reading text	Shared, guided or independent reading of the text (or a similar text type), followed by focused discussion of specific linguistic choices.
Activities on text	Shared or independent activity that consolidates and develops children's understanding of how the text works (may involve sequencing, matching, underlining, etc.).
Creating text	Turning the children's understanding of the text type into writing in shared, guided or independent work. This can focus on any (or all) stages of the writing process from getting ideas to planning or producing a final product.

Figure 9.1 Integrating genre-based work to include talk, reading and writing

These four elements recur in Chapters 3 to 8, but in order to illustrate the principles we will use an example from Chapter 5 on explanations. Work on the sample text 'How the projector works' (pp. 42–3) moves through the following sequence:

- **Talking about the text** – first children discuss their experience of visiting the cinema and think about their existing knowledge of projection. Then they discuss how the sheet might further develop their understanding.
- **Reading the text** – the shared reading of this text draws attention to the interrelationship between the various parts of the projector.
- **Activity on the text** – Photocopiable 1, Projector Quiz, helps children to make a closer reading of the sample text.
- **Creating text** – Photocopiable 3, 'How the bike works', supports children in sequencing an explanation to create a new text.

Extending work on text

While this book has focused on the non-fiction text types highlighted in the National Literacy Strategy Framework of Objectives (DfEE 1998) we have repeatedly stressed that these are primarily school-based genres. We can usefully extend and enrich this work by looking at the roles that other texts play in children's lives.

Television, video and film are important influences in many children's lives. From an early age children are able to identify different genres in these media (Marsh 1999). Video extracts can be used as a stimulus for non-fiction writing or they can be used to prompt discussion about the visual and verbal choices such as those made in the construction of advertisements or news reports. Alternatively, children can be encouraged to experiment with transforming written text types into still and moving images with soundtracks. Recount texts readily lend themselves to this kind of work using a journalistic style, whereas instruction texts can be transformed into a 'Blue Peter television format'.

In a similar way, computers can be used either to support the reading and writing of conventional written texts with word-processing and desktop publishing software, or as a way of exploring new on-screen conventions and text types. We have used some web sources in earlier chapters to illustrate the six text types, but the internet offers a much richer variety of non-fiction texts. Web pages can combine still and moving images, sound files, hypertext and a whole range of new formats (Abbott 1998). Many schools are now introducing children to these text types through their ICT curriculum and some are beginning to involve children in writing web-based material.

New media raise exciting possibilities for text-based work which are beyond the scope of this book. However, it is worth noting here, that these possibilities illustrate the dynamic nature of language and literacy. Televisual and electronic texts show how new conventions emerge and rapidly develop.

As sources of information grow and diversify children will continue to need a good grounding in the literacy of non-fiction and an understanding of the dominant textual forms.

Conclusion

In this chapter we have emphasised the importance of using texts that interest children and are relevant to their everyday life. At the same time we have suggested that, since the six text types are common school-based genres, non-fiction work should be used to make links with different curriculum areas. We have argued for an approach that encourages children to talk about texts, to read them, and to experiment in writing them. Extending non-fiction work will also involve looking at the challenges of working with information sources in new media. In summary:

- **Non-fiction texts should be interesting and relevant to children's lives.**
- **Cross-curricular links are important in developing the use of non-fiction.**
- **Talk, reading and writing all have an important role to play.**
- **Planning for non-fiction needs to acknowledge the diversity and changing nature of information sources.**

Follow the Symbols

This is a key to the symbols used on the map of Historic Eyam and in Photocopiable 2 in Chapter 6.

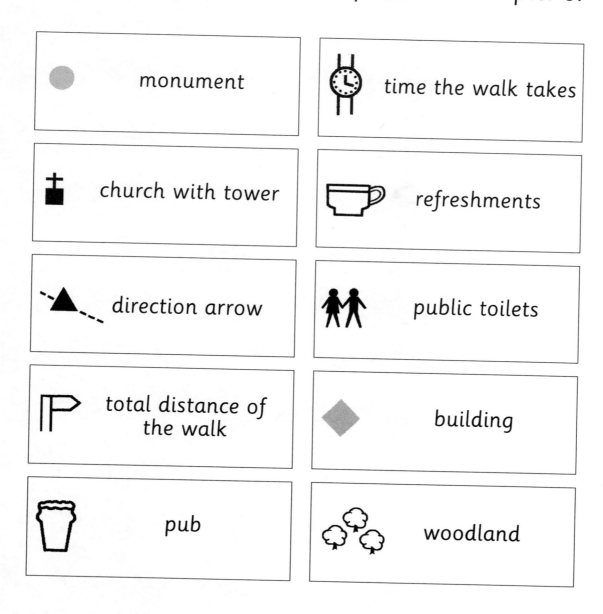

● monument	time the walk takes
church with tower	refreshments
▲ direction arrow	public toilets
total distance of the walk	building
pub	woodland

References

Abbot, C. (1998) 'Making connections: young people and the internet', in Sefton-Green, J. (ed.) *Digital Diversions: Youth Culture in the Age of Multimedia.* London: UCL Press.

Arnold, H. (1996) *Postcards from Kenya.* Winchester: Zoe Books.

Barrs, M. (1994) 'Genre theory: what's it all about?', in Steirer, B. and Maybin, J. (eds) *Language, Literacy and Learning in Educational Practice.* Clevedon: Multilingual Matters/Open University.

Barton, D. and Hamilton, M. (1998) *Local Literacies: Reading and Writing in One Community.* London: Routledge.

Beard, R. (1998) *National Literacy Strategy: Review of Research and other Related Evidence.* Suffolk: DfEE Publications.

Browne, E. (1995) *Handa's Surprise.* London: Walker Books.

Christie, F. (1989) *Language Education.* Oxford: Oxford University Press.

Christie, F. and Misson, R. (1998) 'Framing the issues in literacy education', in Christie, F. and Misson, R. (eds) *Literacy and Schooling.* London: Routledge.

Czerniewska, P. (1992) *Learning about Writing.* Oxford: Blackwell Publishers.

Dadds, M. (1999) 'Teachers' values and the literacy hour', *Cambridge Journal of Education* **29**(1), 7–19.

Derewianka, B. (1991) *Exploring How Texts Work.* Maryborough: Primary English Teaching Association (Australia).

DfEE (1998) *The National Literacy Strategy Framework for Teaching.* London: DfEE.

DfEE (2000) *Grammar for Writing.* London: DfEE.

DfEE (2001) *Developing Early Writing.* London: DfEE.

Education Department of Western Australia (1997) *Writing: Resource Book.* Melbourne: Rigby Heinemann.

Godwin, D. and Perkins, M. (1998) *Teaching Language and Literacy in the Early Years.* London: David Fulton Publishers.

Graves, D. (1983) *Writing: Teachers and Children at Work.* New Hampshire: Heinemann.

Hall, N. (1987) *The Emergence of Literacy.* London: Hodder and Stoughton.

Halliday, M. A. K. and Hasan, R. (1989) *Language, Context and Text: a Social-Semiotic Perspective.* Oxford: Oxford University Press.

Heath, S. B. (1983) *Ways with Words: Language, Life and Work in Communities and Classrooms.* Cambridge: Cambridge University Press.

Kress, G. (1982) *Learning to Write.* London: Routledge and Kegan Paul.

Leeds LEA (1998) *Sustained Reading Intervention.* Leeds: Leeds LEA.

Lewis, M. and Wray, D. (1995) *Developing Children's Non-Fiction Writing.* Leamington Spa: Scholastic.

Lewis, M. and Wray, D. (1997) *Writing Frames.* Reading: Reading and Language Information Centre, The University of Reading.

Littlefair, A. (1991) *Reading all Types of Writing.* Milton Keynes: Open University Press.

Marsh, J. (1999) 'Teletubby tales: popular culture and media education', in Marsh, J. and Hallet, E. (eds) *Desirable Literacies: Approaches to Language and Literacy in the Early Years.* London: Paul Chapman.

Martin, J. R. (1989) *Factual Writing: Exploring and Challenging Social Reality.* Oxford: Oxford University Press.

Meek, M. (1988) *How Texts Teach what Readers Learn.* Stroud: Thimble Press.

Merchant, G. and Thomas, H. (1999) *Picture Books for the Literacy Hour: Activities for Primary Teachers.* London: David Fulton Publishers.

Rimmon-Kenan, S. (1983) *Narrative Fiction: Contemporary Poetics.* London: Routledge.

Roskos, K. and Christie, J. (2001) 'Examining the play–literacy interface: a critical review and future directions', *Journal of Early Childhood Literacy* **1**(1), 59–89.

Taylor, C. (1999) '"I like it when my mum comes to school to work with me": family literacy', in Marsh, J. and Hallet, E. (eds) *Desirable Literacies: Approaches to Language and Literacy in the Early Years.* London: Paul Chapman.

Teale, W. and Sulzby, E. (1986) 'Emergent literacy as a perspective for examining how young children become readers and writers', in Teale, W. and Sulzby, E. (eds) *Emergent Literacy: Writing and Reading.* New Jersey: Ablex.

Tomlinson, T. (1997) *The Cellar Lad.* London: Red Fox.

Webster, A., Beveridge, M. and Reed, M. (1996) *Managing the Literacy Curriculum: How Schools Can Become Communities of Readers and Writers.* London: Routledge.

Wing Jan, L. (1991) *Write Ways: Modelling Writing Forms.* Melbourne: Oxford University Press.

Wray, D. and Lewis, M. (1997) *Extending Literacy: Children Reading and Writing Non-Fiction.* London: Routledge.